SERIOUSLY MEETING KARL SHAPIRO

SERIOUSLY MEETING KARL SHAPIRO

Edited by Sue Walker

Negative Capability Press
Mobile, Alabama
1993

Copyright © 1993 by Negative Capability Press
62 Ridgelawn Drive East
Mobile, Alabama 36608

Manufactured in the United States of America
All rights reserved

Cover: Guillermo de Borja Narvacan IV - "Gumby"

Printer: Thomson-Shore, Inc.

LIBRARY OF CONGRESS CATALOGING-IN-PUBLICATION DATA:
ISBN: 0-942544-19-6

LIBRARY OF CONGRESS CARD NUMBER: 92-093909

PREFACE

It is not uncommon for a graduate student to read voraciously for her qualifying exams, and it was this venture that led me to discover a fondness for Karl Shapiro. I sat in my carrel, *V-Letter* in my hand, and I began to read. I think I opened the book to "Birthday Poem" for I remember thinking that "We are too rich with books, our blood / Is heavy with over-thoughtful food, / Our minds are gravid—and yet to try / To backtrack to simplicity / Is fatal..." reminded me of graduate school, the battleground for a war of minds, a place where students often batter themselves in order to learn so many things they think they'll never know. I was terribly uncomfortable with tapping out iambs and trochees; I thought that the way I said things with a somewhat lingering drawl, that I'd never be able to scan a poem properly. Before I advanced to *Essay on Rime* and *A Prosody Handbook*, however, I had fallen in love with sonnets. I once memorized Edna Millay's "And who are you that missing you . . . ." I was sixteen at the time, zealously in love, and didn't know that the words I committed to memory were the lines of a sonnet. How I chuckled when I read Shapiro's:

I Swore To Stab the Sonnet

> I swore to stab the sonnet with my pen,
> Squash the black widow in a grandstand play
> By gunning down the sonnet form—and then
> I heard you quote my schoolboy love Millay.
> I went to find out what she used to say
> About her tribulations and her men
> And loved her poetry though I now am gray
> And found out love of love poems once again.
> Now I'm the one that's stabbed—son of a bitch!
> With my own poisoned ballpoint pen of love
> And write in sonnet form to make my pitch,
> Words I no longer know the meaning of.
> If I could write one honest sentence now
> I'd say I love you but I don't know how.

I memorized "I Swore To Stab the Sonnet" to dazzle my oral committee, but never found a way to recite the poem. My dazzling recitation remained hidden in some strange convolution of my brain. If I could do it again, I would recite Shapiro and claim that memorizing poetry was an aspect of the qualifying exam.

It never occurred to me then that I would write a letter to Karl Shapiro or that I would start a small press literary journal in 1981. I may not have written him even then, had a friend and fellow grad student, Shameem Choudhury, not dared to send him the first issue. Shapiro responded by saying "*Negative Capability* has a freshness that I like." I waited awhile, then asked Shapiro for a poem to publish in the journal. This was my first letter to him. This time the poet answered "No" with captivating politeness and asked that I "Thank Shameem Choudhury for me for his emblematic poem. It gave me a thrill." The poet went on to explain his refusal. He hadn't been contributing to journals since the publication of his last book.

Almost five years lapsed before another letter was exchanged. Shapiro replied to a new request for a contribution. This time, he sent a poem and added a note of congratulations on the fifth anniversary of *Negative Capability*. There was a postscript: "Don't hesitate to bounce the poem back if you don't cotton to it." As if I would reject Karl Shapiro! Still a gentlemanly "out" was provided, no questions asked.

Two weeks later another letter arrived. Shapiro did what I now think every poet should do when a poem or story is accepted for publication. He writes to express his pleasure in the work's acceptance.

"May I keep the xerox of the proof", he adds. "It's a nice souvenir." What genuine niceness, courtesy—how Shapiro!

It is some time later that Karl Shapiro agrees to be one of the journals Advisory Editors, but he expresses reservations about an issue—a festschrift, in his honor. He doesn't like "tooting his horn all over the lot," he says. He digresses, answers a question posed to him about sonnets: "The iambic should be, has to be contradicted by natural speech.I try to just make sure the underlying meter is only scotched not killed. . . ." Karl Shapiro, the instructor, instructs. He does not pontificate.

I wish that I could have been Ted Kooser who writes about Karl Shapiro in the early sixties. I wish I could have enrolled in his writing course and the lecture class on contemporary poetry. But I am blessed to know Karl Shapiro's gentleness. When my father dies, and I write and convey this news, he answers: "Nothing is harder to convey than condolences. But an elder can send blessings."

A year or so ago, I had the opportunity to visit Karl and his delightful, wonderful wife Sophie at their home in Davis. I was busy planning this festschrift. It is a small way to say thank you, Karl— for your poetry, for your support of poets and publishing, for the many blessings you have given. And thank you, Sophie, for the rose you picked and gave me as I left. Its petals are potpourri now: the scent of roses.

Sue Walker, Mobile, Alabama, April 1993

CONTENTS

Sue Walker	Preface	
John Updike	Homage to Karl	1
Hayden Carruth	A Salute In Time	3
Leo Connellan	Ode To Karl Shapiro	6
A. Duckworth	Karl Shapiro's University And The Ideology Of Place	10
Leo Haber	About Karl Shapiro	28
Joseph Harris	The Towing Of The Poetry Wreck	29
Ted Kooser	Karl Shapiro In The Early Sixties	30
J.T. Ledbetter	Shapiro: Three Memories	34
Glenna Luschei	Originals	35
	Machine	36
	Giraffe Or Scholars	37
Jim Lynch	Karl Shapiro: Six Decades of Per-Verse	38
James E. Miller, Jr.	Karl Shapiro in Nebraska	45
John F. Nims	Spontaneous Effusion In Honor Of Karl Shapiro	48
	The Early Years	51
Hans Ostrom	"This Isn't A Poem Yet": Karl Shapiro The Teacher	62
Louis D. Rubin	Poet In Eclipse	66
Robert Phillips	A National Monument	69
David R. Slavitt	An Homage And A Poem To Karl	72
John Wheatcroft	Love And War	77
Peter Viereck	On Karl Shapiro	79
Ken Stone	Phenomenon	80
	Worship	81

John Brugaletta	Sacrifice	82
Robert Phillips	Karl Shapiro And His Latest Poems	83
Sophie Wilkins	Seriously Meeting Karl Shapiro	89
Karl Shapiro	Notes On Raising A Poet	109
	Virginia Beach	131
Sue Walker	Drinking Iron Kuan Yin With Karl Shapiro	132

PHOTOGRAPHS

Norfolk, Va, about 1918 99

Baltimore, 1941 100

Sydney, Australia, 1942 101

Hopkins Professor, 1948 102

With T.S. Eliot 103

Cherry Blossoms 104

Real Speech, Real Life 105

Karl Shapiro, 1979 106

Where Thoughts Sip Peace And Garden 107

I Dreamed I Held A Poem And Knew 108

NOTES ON CONTRIBUTORS 133
ACKNOWLEDGEMENTS 137

~KS~
John Updike
HOMAGE TO KARL

I first encountered the work of Karl Shapiro in *The New Yorker* of the 1940s, and then, at college, in *The Oxford Book of American Verse* as edited by F. O. Matthiessen in 1950. Coming after (in the collection) the loose egoistic effusions of Delmore Schwartz and shortly before the knotty pentameters of the early Robert Lowell, Shapiro's poems recognizably belonged to this world, to my America, with curt declarative titles like "Midnight Show," "Hollywood," "Nigger," and "Drug Store." From "Drug Store":

> It baffles the foreigner like an idiom,
> And he is right to adopt it as a form
> Less serious than the living-room or bar;
> For it disestablishes the café,
> Is a collective, and on basic country.
>
> . . .
>
> Youth comes to jingle nickels and crack wise;
> The baseball scores are his, the magazines,
> Devoted to lust, the jazz, the Coca-Cola,
> The lending-library of love's latest.
> He is the customer; he is heroized.

And, not included by Matthiessen but somehow remembered by me, "Auto Wreck" with the beautiful opening lines

> Its quick soft silver bell beating, beating,
> And down the dark one ruby flare
> Pulsing out red light like an artery,
> The ambulance at top speed floating down ...

and "A Cut Flower" with its stunning last questions "Where are my bees? Must I die now? Is this part of life?" and his soldier's

"Homecoming" with its horribly factual

> We bring no raw materials from the East
> But green-skinned men in blue-lit holds
> And lunatics impounded between-decks....

These were songs of experience, experience I could recognize even where I had not shared it. They were just, in the sense in which Richard Wilbur has described Sylvia Plath's poems as "unjust," and the sense in which Lowell's images of America were unjust—complaining, nagging, scornful. Shapiro has Whitman's good nature, and his wide embrace. In his remarkably relaxed memoirs, even where complaints might be justified—he was enlisted in the Eliot-led campaign to give the Jew-hating Pound the Bollingen Prize, and finally rebelled and protested; his poetry was entirely dropped by Richard Ellmann from *The New Oxford Book of American Verse* —his accounts are mild, fair-minded, delivered with a shrug. As keen and amused an observer of himself as of anyone else, he gives us personal testimony moderated, defused, made limp and light, by an impersonal calm; he has a touch of southern courtliness left over, perhaps, from his Baltimore upbringing. Recent poems of his express bemusement about himself as a lover and as a Jew—two roles in which most speakers would not dare diffidence. In his poetry, he has taken an unfashionable direction, backwards toward the Beats, toward the days of long-lined personal explosion. "All things remain to be simplified. I find I must break free of the poetry trap," he writes in his Rimbaudesque cascade "I Am an Atheist Who Says His Prayers." He has turned to prose poems, to prosy poems to unburden himself of awkward truths. His is an America endured without a grudge, wherein the poet, like the tourist of "Washington Cathedral," is "only a good alien, nominally happy." Bless Shapiro for his modest immodesty, his continuing verbal adventurism, his honest bemusement, his incorrigible sanity.

~ KS ~
Hayden Carruth
A SALUTE IN TIME

Old people wish they could somehow recreate the quality of their early experience, because they feel that this is a value in the world, a value slipping away and yet needed. But of course such recreation is not possible. The quality of yesterday is already gone, and that of forty years ago—well, it could be four hundred years ago. And this is part of the sadness and sense of loss that pervade all our lives.

Teachers will know how I feel when I say that I am appalled by my own repeated failure to give my students an emotional awareness of the near past that they cannot possibly apprehend.

When I first read Karl Shapiro's *Person, Place, and Thing* (1942), which was his first full-fledged book of poems, I was excited by it in a way that I never had been before. It may have been the first book by a contemporary that I had encountered; I don't remember clearly. But I do remember how fresh, new, vigorous, and pointed the poems were, how they awakened me to whole perspectives of poetic possibility that I had never suspected before. Here were poems taken from the American actuality I knew, from the technological world, cars, radios, industrial blight, the terrifying impersonality of death from machines. Other American writers had been literary Realists and Naturalists, of course; but writers like Sandburg, Anderson, even Hemingway, even such "proletarian pets" as Kenneth Fearing and Langston Hughes, seemed to me spoiled by sentimentality. Nothing like that could be found in Shapiro's poems about totaled cars and smashed houses. No weakness at all.

All the poems were beautiful. I had always felt an impulse, a powerful one, toward the work of Alexander Pope and other neo-classical poets, an impulse which I had felt I must suppress in the face of the overwhelming romanticist bias of my teachers and fellow students. But here was a poet, a contemporary, writing beautiful poems in a manner that I instantly recognized, the beauty of good, hard, varied meters and tough, functional rhymes. Appropriateness: that's what hit me, I suppose. I was excited, and I wasn't the only one. When Shapiro's second major collection was published, *V-Letter and Other Poems* (1944), though it was not quite as good as his first, it was awarded the Pulitzer Prize. I had written a good many v-letters myself during the war, and I knew the fear, bewilderment, loneliness, and boredom that were so well brought forth in Shapiro's poems. Later I encountered Jarrell's war poems and Tom McGrath's and others'; but with me and with many young people in those days Shapiro's were first.

Shortly afterward, *Essay on Rime* came out, Shapiro's book length poem about poetry. Again the crispness and appropriateness of the writing took hold of me powerfully, and the acuteness of the theoretical concepts. Between Pope's *Essay on Criticism* and the present, only Shapiro has produced an essay in verse worth reading, and I wish more people would pay attention to it.

Of course we knew that Shapiro had been influenced by Auden and other English poets of the Oxford group. But it was an influence we could celebrate. Shapiro was derivative but never imitative. He was American. None of that twiddly lah-de-dah we could detect—or thought we could—in even the most stringent poems by Auden and Spender. It made all the difference. And when Shapiro went on to rebel against not only prevailing literary attitudes but his own tastes and styles, as he did several times, we applauded. In *Poems of a Jew* (1958) we welcomed the new lyrical quality, somewhat Yeatsian but again definitely of the New World, and the prosaic poetry of *The Bourgeois Poet* (1964) seemed to us quite wonderful in the way it hit a rebellious tone that was not like Whitman or Williams or the Beats, but something new and different. Perhaps it reminded us of such French poets as St. John Perse or Francis Ponge, a clear and powerful, incisive language that was new in American English.

In 1946 when I was a graduate student at the University of Chicago, I had a few poems accepted by *Poetry*. I was as green as a new poet could be. One day I was walking down a corridor at the university and looked up to see Shapiro approaching me, accompanied by Judith Bond, who was the university's librarian in charge of contemporary poetry. I knew she would introduce me. I was pathologically shy, however, and my instinct was to turn aside, to escape; but I couldn't: there was no place to escape to. When Mrs. Bond stopped me and introduced me, Shapiro told me that he was visiting Chicago and had just had lunch with the staff at *Poetry*. He had been shown my poems in manuscript, he said, and he liked them a good deal. This was my first meeting with a well-known writer, someone whom I could recognize from his photos on the dust covers of his books. I can't say that this was what confirmed me in my desire to become a poet—who can be sure of the truth about such things forty years later?—but I can say very positively that it easily might be the truth, that it certainly is part of the truth.

Shapiro's more recent work, the lovely "Aubade" and the other erotic poems of the past fifteen years or so, seem to me altogether fine and fitting, though again they are a departure from the poetry he had written earlier. Shapiro's poetic courage, his willingness to change, his insistence on it, has been a great example. Similarly his criticism, especially *In Defense of Ignorance* (1960), which contains some outrageous judgements, has been determinative for me. In fact the two critics who have influenced me most during my lifetime have both been men whose particular judgments often offended me, Yvor Winters and Karl Shapiro. With criticism the *intention* is what counts, and both men in their anger wrote with a selfless, enthusiastic devotion to artistic values that carries more weight than mere judiciousness. But most of all I learned from Shapiro that you can look out your window and make a poem from what you see. You not only can, you must. This is the responsible poet's obligation. All else is bluffing. No one has demonstrated this more convincingly than Karl Shapiro in all his work.

~ KS ~
Leo Connellan

ODE TO KARL SHAPIRO

Along the Hudson and Westchester
the lone heterosexual rides in his last maiden
into her screaming dawn.

From now on she'll be known as all knowing
liberated woman who doesn't give anything to you,
and doesn't want anything.

Your size means nothing to her and
what you can do with it, nothing and
it means very little to her if she does it,
and very little if she doesn't.

The city of New York is cracked. Where the moon rises
Karl Shapiro lands at Idlewild. Along Broadway
Jack Dempsey's is become th' home of th' Whopper
and George M. Cohan finally looks ridiculous
in Pigeon expression.

From the jungles of the South Pacific pulling
detail on Pacific isles, came home Karl Shapiro
with Bill Mauldin and Ernie Pyle, everybody's
cartoonist, everybody's drinking buddy correspondent,
and a poet who was in a war.

Karl Shapiro home like the Lion of Judah on
the pages of the *New Yorker*, put a Pulitzer in
his pocket and to Chicago, edited, then
Japan, India, Germany, Nebraska ... California.

Along the Hudson and Westchester the
highway broke apart and fell down on
pier scurrying thieves underneath.

The old west side trail crushed from
trucks, taxi cabs and motorists weaving
in and out in sudden death hurry.

Drenching the air in sweat and gas
while a thousand shady deals cost lives
and it cost your life to try and stay alive.

In the dawn moon the lone heterosexual
rides his last maiden singing "Hi-Ho
Blonde Chick aw-waay!" and swinging Edsel
landed at Kennedy.

Karl Shapiro, I sing to you from my youth for
your great courage when you didn't have to and
it would have profited you more not to stand up
against the WASP and the FASCIST.

But this will not be one-a' them revealing tributes,
in which I cry "This one, too, Karl, this one,
too, is a bisexual faggot under the skin!" ... or
"Hey, Karl, bebbe, whachoo doin' down there
among th' Irish?"

When this nobody came to you, you who were everything
embraced me. I have only imagined poems,
you, Karl, have written them.

What it was to read your images! Freeing us
from Whitman long before Allen told us it was
all right to tongue somebody's ear out, you wrote
"Buick" and "Nigger" while Federico saw
butterflies in Walt's beard and, excited,
a youngster, I wrote....

                TO BEGIN WITH

But my years now
in half seconds each squeezed for the utmost.
Defeated House Invalid's complete ceasing.
Fire the Pilot Light in the furnace of myself

like one kneeling outdoors on a windy night
presses lips close to the new starting fire,
softly blows it to re-kindle where the spark had died.

And, swimming in my head your "Buick," Karl, I wrote then,
STAY LOOSE
When the rent man comes frothing into your pig-sty
eyes throwing you out, and the rat you've been sharing with
tip-toes cross door ledge behind him refusing to spring
bite into his roast beef fed neck that his face juts off
like a constipated owl, as his drool hangs at the crevice
where a chin, somewhere in the rolls of greasy flesh should
be,
ask him back. Be a host who's too busy to see a sick friend,
while his look pops disbelief as he can't catch his breath.
Push him back in that hall an animal would go blind in.
Gently slamming the door and bending, shove through
to his greedy little reach an envelope on which is scribbled,
small as a needle point ... I'm moving ... soon ... soon.

along the Hudson and Westchester
that road has broken off with us.

And downtown the chortling clowns
hustle us, Karl, out of our literature.

Second rate mediocrity arriving to read
what they call their "poems" on stages
like The New School, nasty mean people
always lugging knapsacks bent over like
the crawling things they are, struggling, not
about poetry but careers, what will be bad
enough not to threaten and so allowed.

There may be no Schliemann to find
the lost Troy of verse, Karl, and no
one who even knows Delmore Schwartz.
No one who reads Eberhart and Jarrell,

Leo Connellan

Allen's Kaddish or the Federico
Watermelon poem or who ever
heard of the Naomi Replansky.

But, Karl Shapiro, I sing to you for standing
for these people and these things. I sing
to you for myself because you gave me
myself in my art and you gave me yourself.

Alistair M. Duckworth

Karl Shapiro's "University" and the Ideology of Place

The publication in 1988 of *The Younger Son*, the first volume of Karl Shapiro's autobiography, confirms what many have known or strongly suspected: that the subject of "University" is the University of Virginia in Charlottesville. Born in 1913, Shapiro attended UVA for a semester in 1932, experiencing there the prejudice and elitism he bitterly registers in the poem. In *Younger Son*, Shapiro describes how he was persuaded against entitling the poem "University of Virginia" by his brother, who had recently graduated from the university with highest honors. He also describes the incident that sparked the poem, which was a snub from two "upper-class Jews" who had been his best friends in high school in Norfolk (139-40). That the specific anti-semitic occasion of the poem should have been an insult to a Russian Jew by two German Jews is surprising; but that the poem is a response to a much broader milieu of discrimination and prejudice is clear in what follows:

The entire University of Virginia was a social hierarchy, beginning with the FFV's, the First Families of Virginia, and ending with the Blacks, who were not of course allowed to attend the University at all.... But Jews could be admitted. The Virginia and in fact all the Southern aristocracy would not tolerate common anti-Semitism; that was ungentlemanly. The poet remembered how once he had been introduced at a Virginia party by the hostess as "this nice Hebrew gentleman." As he brooded on the poem, it became clearer and clearer that he was writing about Virginia and himself as rejected suitor, rejected even by the upper-class German Jews whose great-grandfathers had fought in the Confederacy for the Stars and Bars, while his ancestors were still being pillaged and murdered in Russian-Polish villages and ghettoes (140).

Shapiro's "stern and colorful condemnation of the famous school" (*Younger Son*, 139) did not appear immediately. He composed "University" some six or seven years later while attending Johns Hopkins University (1937-39); it was accepted by *Poetry* in October 1940 and then appeared in *Person, Place and Thing* in 1942. In *Younger Son*, Shapiro notes that soon after its appearance in *Poetry* the poem was reprinted in the student magazine at the University of Virginia, that it remained popular with the students, and that it did not seem to damage his reputation with the faculty (141). Further mitigation of the oppositional force of "University" appears, curiously enough, in #64, section XV of *The Bourgeois Poet*, where Shapiro writes:

> Purely out of boredom I involve others in "a question of principle." I defame the University in passing. Then I allow myself to be persuaded to withdraw the accusations (which are valid). I apologize to the conspirators, not to the injured.

Shapiro's comments here are disconcerting; and the account of his retraction (with reservations) is perhaps explained by his ambivalent feelings toward the University of Virginia; even now, he admits he has "never gotten over [his] semester at the U. of VA. and keep[s] a picture of the Lawn ... on [his] bulletin board" (personal letter)[1]. But if we wish to recover the poem's radical force—to discover in it "that special savagery of attack" which, in Allen Tate's view, distinguished *Person, Place and Thing* as a whole—we need only set it in the context of his later condemnations of elitism, prejudice, and anti-semitism.[2] In 1949, Shapiro (along with Irving Howe, Harry Levin, Lionel Trilling, and other prominent Jewish writers) contributed to a symposium in *Commentary* on "The Jewish Writer and the English Literary Tradition." In his response, Shapiro did not temporize, as Harry Levin, for example, did when he sought to contextualize negative representations of the Jew in English literature. Calling on American Jewish intellectuals and poets to create a "counter mythos" to "the literary myth of the Bestial Jew," he stated that "if I do not believe in a new and separate American civilization, I shall have no other cultural identity" (369-70). In 1958, he published *Poems of a Jew*; and in 1960, he published *In Defense of Ignorance*, a collection of essays that included pieces vigorously objecting to the dominant influence of T. S. Eliot and Ezra Pound on American poets, as well as an essay entitled "W. B. Yeats: Trial by Culture," and another in which—against the dominance of Eliot, Pound and Yeats—he nominated

William Carlos Williams as "the true contemporary." In all this, a pattern emerges of a writer who—made to feel an exile in his own land—was determined to combat the English, and more generally European, usurpation of American culture. Unlike Lionel Trilling who, in his study of E. M. Forster (1943), conducted a not so veiled attack on contemporary American literature for its failure to enter into dialogue with the great books of the (European) past, Shapiro sought (in Williams's phrase) a "homemade world." Like Malcolm Cowley who, in *Exile's Return* (1934), recalled how small town boys at Harvard were instructed in the literary rites of the international scene, while being stripped of their local accents, dress, and associations (29-39), he deplored the enculturation of American youth into a traditionalism that was as much social as literary in character. Like Cowley—and like Delmore Schwartz, too, at Harvard in the thirties—Shapiro knew that a university could be a place, not only of anti-semitism, but of cultural indoctrination; and in *Person, Place and Thing*, typically, he described places that were popular rather than polite, American rather than English, even as he found in Auden—a poet who had famously reversed Eliot's journey across the Atlantic—an alternative model of style, rhythm, and diction. In his *Nation* review, Delmore Schwartz praised Shapiro's style: "the literary feat of the volume," Schwartz noted, "is that of taking the style of Auden and transforming it with an American subject matter, by writing of drugstores, lunch wagons, a conscription camp, a midnight show, a Buick, and many other things equally indigenous" (63). Understandably, Schwartz has nothing to say of "University," which does not fit this bill at all. In *Younger Son*, Shapiro tells of how he made up the formal stanzaic structure of "University" (139). In one sense, his poetic formalism is a tribute to the university itself, "the American place he thought most beautiful," as he admits in *Younger Son* (139). The formal features of the poem—its five stanzas, each comprising four lines of pentameters, followed by three tetrameters, and one dimeter; the formal diction; the weighty adjectives—mimic the appearance of the architecture on the Lawn at the University of Virginia, even as they successively treat the place, the students, the faculty, the "luckless race" in the nearby hills, and Jefferson himself on "his private mountain." In another sense, however, the formal features of the poem, together with its coded imagery, are a way of subverting from within the ideology which the setting represents. Like other descriptions of buildings and landscapes in literature, "University" is an extended metonym whose value-laden terms combine to signify social and political meanings. But whereas a poet like Yeats, or a novelist like Henry James, endorses the traditional values signified by particular settings, Shapiro inscribes these values in order to expose and undercut them. What seems natural is, in fact, cultural, and what seems harmonious conceals prejudice and exploitation. In this way, though he may not yet have formulated his intention, he is already engaged in writing, around 1939, the countermythos he called for in the *Commentary* symposium in 1949. In the reading that follows the poem, I shall support this proposal, first by observing the specificity of Shapiro's notations, and then by pursuing one of the poem's tangents into the cultural tradition—which is also the textual field—that he condemned and opposed.

University

To hurt the Negro and avoid the Jew
Is the curriculum. In mid-September
The entering boys, identified by hats,
Wander in a maze of mannered brick
    Where boxwood and magnolia brood
    And columns with imperious stance
    Like rows of ante-bellum girls
    Eye them, outlanders.

In whited cells, on lawns equipped for peace,
Under the arch, and lofty banister,
Equals shake hands, unequals blankly pass;
The exemplary weather whispers, "Quiet, quiet"
    And visitors on tiptoe leave
    For the raw North, the unfinished West,
    As the young, detecting an advantage,
    Practice a face.

Where, on their separate hill, the colleges,
Like manor houses of an older law,
Gaze down embankments on a land in fee,

> The Deans, dry spinsters over family plate,
> Ring out the English name like coin,
> Humor the snob and lure the lout.
> Within the precincts of this world
> Poise is a club.
>
> But on the neighboring range, misty and high,
> The past is absolute: some luckless race
> Dull with inbreeding and conformity
> Wears out its heart, and comes barefoot and bad
> For charity or jail. The scholar
> Sanctions their obsolete disease;
> The gentleman revolts with shame
> At his ancestor.
>
> And the true nobleman, once a democrat,
> Sleeps on his private mountain. He was one
> Whose thought was shapely and whose dream was
>   broad;
> This school he held his art and epitaph.
> But now it takes from him his name,
> Falls open like a dishonest look,
> And shows us rotted and endowed,
> Its senile pleasure.

If, in the first stanza, boxwood, magnolia, and "columns with imperious stance / Like rows of ante-bellum girls" are general codes of the American South, other details are more specific. In the last stanza the "true nobleman" is surely Jefferson and the "private mountain" on which he sleeps is the hill on which he built Monticello. Reading back from here, one sees that the "whited cells" and "lawns equipped for peace" in the second stanza must refer respectively to the students' rooms behind the colonnades and to the lawn that stretches down from the Rotunda, Jefferson's scaled-down version of the Roman Pantheon. The lawn, still so named (it is a solecism at the University of Virginia to refer to the "campus"), is bordered on each side by five elegant pavilions, creative variations on Palladian models. And if the whited cells—without central heating until recently—have always been prized by Virginia students since the days that Edgar Allan Poe attended the university, then the pavilions have been traditionally the homes of distinguished professors or deans—those "dry spinsters over family plate" who, in Shapiro's view, "humor the snob and lure the lout." Moreover, one of the pavilions is the Colonnade Club, which gives intentional ambiguity to Shapiro's "poise is a club" at the end of the third stanza. In the fourth stanza, "the neighboring range, misty and high" is the Blue Ridge mountains, the most easterly of the Appalachian ranges, about twenty miles west of Charlottesville. The university, then, is the University of Virginia, and its curriculum is "to hurt the Negro and avoid the Jew." But if the referent in the poem seems to be as unambiguous as the attack on prejudice is overt and bitter, the poem raises certain questions—questions that begin and end with the paradox that an ideal democratic place has become an abode of snobbery and discrimination.

The University of Virginia, Mr. Jefferson's Academical Village, built at his initiative and largely to his designs between 1817 and 1826, is often viewed as America's finest architectural ensemble (in 1976 the American Institute of Architects recognized it as "the proudest achievement of American architecture since 1776"). Before Stanford White, at the beginning of this century, erected a classroom building, the vista from the Rotunda looked down the lawn and out into the country, where Monticello stood on its hill. As Shapiro indicates in the last stanza, Jefferson was proud of his creation, and in his epitaph chose to describe himself—not as a two-term President of the United States but—as "author of the Declaration of Independence, of the Statute of Virginia for religious freedom, and father of the University of Virginia."

In the university of the 1930s, however, the ideals of Jefferson, "the true nobleman, once a democrat," have degenerated and become corrupt. The democracy in question here is perhaps not so much the Republican principles Jefferson opposed to Hamilton's Federalist attempts to create a strong central executive, but rather the kind of democracy that Jefferson exhibited when, as President, typically dressed in plain cloth, he refused to have any truck with precedence, titles, diplomatic grades, or other distinctive signs of class difference. Knowing that political power perpetuates itself through theatrical behavior as well as through political and legal institutions, Jefferson as President opposed the hegemony of the aristocracy at the level of dress and ceremony no less than in his earlier statutes of reform that repealed the law of entail and eradicated primogeniture in the Virginia constitution. Ironical, then, that in the university of the 1930s dress and ceremony are once more instruments of power (the freshmen are identified by hats; "equals shake hands," whereas "unequals blankly pass"). Ironical, too, that the ideals Jefferson espoused—of America for Americans, for example, or of the provision of an egalitarian system of education—have been betrayed; his school "falls open like a dishonest look," and the Deans, false to their American heritage, "ring out the *English* name like coin" (emphasis added). I shall return to this sense of "English" as the currency of discrimination later. Like the use of Palladian architecture by English Whigs earlier in the eighteenth century, Jefferson's brilliant appropriation of Palladian architecture may have been intended to communicate a Republican message. But in the 1930s the lawn signifies a different meaning to the poet. Now its architecture seems complicit in the aristocratic ideology being repudiated. The freshmen "wander in a maze of *mannered brick*"; the boxwood, magnolia, and the Palladian columns are "imperious" and threatening. Between the time of Jefferson and the time of Shapiro the Civil War and Reconstruction have intervened, and these events doubtless explain in part why an architecture originally Republican in intent has become aristocratic and exclusive. But there is more to Shapiro's distrust of buildings and grounds than this, and the more has to do with literary history rather than social history. It is not wrong, I think, to hear in the first line of the second stanza echoes of Yeats—the Yeats of such poems as "Ancestral Houses," "Coole Park and Ballylee," "A Prayer for My Daughter":

> Surely among a rich man's flowering lawns,
> Amid the rustle of his planted hills,
> Life overflows without ambitious pains ...(198)

In a later poem, entitled "The Southerner," Shapiro writes of "the nonsense of the gracious lawn" (*Collected Poems*, 107), and, again, the line has a double reference—to an actual South, to a literary code.

Yeats's allegiance to the Anglo-Irish landed order—in whose custom and ceremony he found a political base and the "grounds" of future hope—has, I suggest, colored Shapiro's negative assessment of the grace and proportion of the university's architecture and of the peace and harmony of its grounds, where even the exemplary September weather is somehow threatening. [3] What is being attacked, then, in the poem is certainly a specific place—the university where Shapiro was made to feel an "outlander"—but it is also a code of representation—the code of the ancestral house or (to cite the phrase of that expatriate American Henry James, who also made extensive use of the code) of "the great good place." By positing the intervention of such a code, at any rate, it is possible to understand the force of the otherwise curious comparison Shapiro makes at the beginning of the third stanza:

> Where, on their separate hill, the colleges,
> *Like manor houses of an older law,*
> Gaze down embankments on a land in fee....
> (emphasis added)

With few exceptions, the college buildings of the University of Virginia continue the Jeffersonian tradition of looking to Rome and Greece for architectural inspiration, and it could doubtless be argued that they resemble existing manor houses in Virginia. David King Gleason's sumptuous *Virginia Plantation Homes*, which contains photographs of the University of Virginia, also contains photographs of houses that Shapiro might have had in mind in making his comparison (Jefferson's own Monticello is one possiblility; Farmington in Charlottesville, which became a country club in 1927, but remains an example of an eighteenth-century Piedmont plantation house, is another). [4] I assume, however, that "manor houses of the older law" refers generally to the code of the English manor house and not to any specific site in England or Virginia; the adjective "English" appears in the same stanza, almost precisely at the center of the poem. Though English manor houses may during the Georgian period be of Palladian design, they tend to antedate the Palladian revivals in architecture of the seventeenth and eighteenth centuries; the manor houses of the literary tradition are medieval, Tudor, or Jacobean in origin, and are usually characterized by a mixture of architectural styles. Typical is Compton Wynates, the Warwickshire house Henry James described (1877) in panegyrical fashion in *English Hours* (148-49).

Descriptions of such houses exist in great abundance in the novels of Scott, Austen, Trollope, James, and others. Like the houses illustrated in Joseph Nash's *Mansions of England in the Olden Time* (1839-49), manor houses in English fiction are usually occasions for rhetorical praise. Their fictional function is metonymic; they give physical form to ideas of heritage, tradition, rootedness, cultural continuity; the values they accommodate are those of hospitality, charity, good-housekeeping, communal life. Such neo-feudal (or "English") values are precisely what Shapiro discovers—and deplores—in the Charlottesville of the thirties, which he describes as a "land in fee," a land in which "some luckless race / ... Wears out its heart, and comes barefoot and bad / For charity or jail."

In order to specify the power of place to promote traditional values, and to identify—in one of its manifestations—the ideology against which Shapiro wrote, I shall now refer to Jane Austen's description of Donwell Abbey in *Emma* (1816). It is a famous description, not least because of the attention Lionel Trilling devoted to it in his essay on the novel; in *Emma*, Trilling noted Austen's "tendency to conceive of a specifically English ideal of life" (40).[5] True, Shapiro had not read *Emma* when he wrote "University"(personal communication); and my collocation of Austen's description with his may therefore seem strained. The justification for yoking Shapiro and Austen together—a thing unattempted yet in prose or rhyme—must emerge in my subsequent argument; but I should make it clear that the connection is not a question of source and influence but of writers using traditional settings to mediate their distinctive relations to society and history. Shapiro's university and Austen's abbey are not the strange neighbors they might at first seem; instead, they are buildings in the same (textual) countryside, and secret pathways run between them, as well as—I shall shortly argue—between them and other texts, including T. S. Eliot's. Shapiro and Austen are both concerned with questions of manors and manners—of property and propriety—and while they come to different conclusions, their arguments are mutually illuminating.

Donwell Abbey is the home of Mr. Knightley (significantly named if ever a fictional character was), and its cultural value is communicated to us through the heroine's perspective on the occasion of the strawberry party, staged by the officious Mrs. Elton, interloper on the Highbury scene:

> [Emma] felt all the honest pride and complacency which her alliance with the present and future proprietor could fairly warrant, as she viewed the respectable size and style of the building, its suitable, becoming, characteristic situation, low and sheltered—its ample gardens . . . its abundance of timber in rows and avenues. . . . The house was . . . rambling and irregular. . . . It was just what it ought to be and it looked what it was—and Emma felt an increasing respect for it, as the residence of a family of such true gentility, untainted in blood and understanding. (358)

Austen's description is a brief anthology of codes of representation marshalled in the interests of a conservative social vision. The abundant trees, the low and sheltered situation, especially the "irregular" house, signify ideas of heritage and tradition. Donwell Abbey is Shapiro's "manor house of the older law," and as in Shapiro's poem, it may be said to "gaze down embankments on a land in fee." Near the end of the strawberry party led by the *arriviste* Mrs. Elton, "in all her apparatus of happiness," the group in the Donwell Abbey grounds, now dispersed and irritable, come to a place from where an "extremely pretty" view may be enjoyed:

> . . . at half a mile distant was a bank of considerable abruptness and grandeur, well clothed with wood;—and at the bottom of this bank, favourably placed and sheltered, rose the Abbey-Mill Farm, with meadows in front, and the river making a close and handsome curve around it. It was a sweet view—sweet to the eye and the mind. English verdure, English culture, English comfort, seen under a sun bright, without being oppressive. (360)

Jane Austen is remarkably frank in her chauvinism. Alerted by Roland Barthes's *Mythologies*, we expect ideologies to be hidden in texts; in their ideological aspects texts signify not directly but at one remove; and the suspicious critic's role is to uncover the ideological signified beneath the realistic signifier—to show, in fact, that realism is never more than a code of representation. No need to do that here: Austen gives us the signifier—the view of the Abbey-Mill farm—and then the signified—English culture. Here is the view, she says, and this is what it means. And if the philologist should remind us that "culture" in the present context means "agriculture," we would be quite justified in replying that while agriculture is signified at one level—the representational—culture is signified at a second level—the ideological.

The description of the Abbey-Mill farm comes at an important moment in the novel. In the next chapter is the Box Hill episode, during which Emma, in collusion with Frank Churchill, insults Miss Bates, poor, single, and dependent. Mr. Knightley reproaches Emma for her rudeness, and Emma, realizing the enormity of her action, repents. In the chapters that follow Emma realizes she is in love with Mr. Knightley; and as Emma, the heiress, becomes mistress of Donwell Abbey, so Jane Fairfax, accomplished but penniless, is able to marry Frank Churchill on the fortuitous death of Frank's rich aunt, and Harriet Smith, the illegitimate daugher of "nobody knows whom" (61) is rewarded with Robert Martin, Mr. Knightley's tenant farmer at the Abbey-Mill farm, whom Emma had once considered unworthy of her. Trilling, by the way, considered that Emma's early dismissal of the worthy Mr. Martin to be of nothing less than "national import" in the novel (40). Like setting, plot supports Austen's traditional views of society by ensuring that the female characters make "equal" matches and discover their "natural" partners.

Jane Austen's ideal society is not—any more than the weather at Donwell Abbey—oppressive. It is a society which rejects aristocratic arrogance, on the one side, and is hospitable to individual merit when it appears in energetic yeomen like Robert Martin or businessmen like Mr. Cole, on the other. But it is also a society that accepts, even promotes, the existence of social rankings, a society in which, socially as well as scenically, the manor "looks down" on the farm, and a society that is—insistently—"English."

The oppositions which emerge in an intertextual comparison of Austen and Shapiro may now be summarized: whereas in *Emma* setting and weather (even in England!) combine to connote idealized "English" values that ask for the reader's assent, in "University" setting and weather conspire to connote anachronistic "English" values that demand the reader's repudiation. In the novel the heroine is at home in her culture; she is, if you like, an inlander; in the poem, on the other hand, the speaker is an alien in the university to which he has come, an outlander. The novel—or, to be more cautious, a dominant voice in the novel—calls for the perpetuation of traditional values, for the maintenance of a "moral economy" and for an acceptance of an inherited social structure—however open that society may be to certain kinds of deserving initiative. The poem bitterly regrets that traditional values—the older law of the manor, entailing paternalist and patriarchal assumptions—have returned to the university and the state from which Jefferson had uprooted them.

I should stress again that no argument is being made here for any direct connection between the two texts being considered. What I do argue is that their juxtaposition leads to a mutual illumination of textual meanings. Enough perhaps has been said to show that Shapiro's poem is not simply an attack on the prejudice existing at the University of Virginia in the 1930s; it is also an attack on the English literary tradition, and, more particularly, on the migratory code of the ancestral house found in Yeats's poetry and, before Yeats, in English fiction, of which *Emma* is here taken only as an instance. Shapiro is drawn to his attack because he recognizes the anti-democratic force of the code.

He may, in fact, have had a particular reason for his animus. Though T. S. Eliot's Page-Barbour Lectures at the University of Virginia were delivered in April 1933, shortly after Shapiro's departure from Charlottesville, he would surely have read them—sooner or later—in their printed form. [6] *After Strange Gods: A Primer of Modern Heresy* was published in 1934, and in its general defence of orthodoxy, and even more in its particular formulations, it contains enough to have infuriated Shapiro. "You have here," Eliot proposed to his Charlottesville audience, "at least some recollection of a 'tradition,' such as the influx of foreign populations has almost effaced in some parts of the North, and such as never established itself in the West" (15). (Shapiro's visitors to the university, we recall, leave for "the raw North, the unfinished West.") Eliot continues: "What is still more important [to the maintenance of tradition] is unity of religious background; and reasons of race and religion combine to make any large number of free-thinking Jews undesirable" (20). Eliot later disavowed *After Strange Gods* and refused to reprint it; in 1933, however, his attacks on individualism and 'personality' continued the arguments of his immensely influential "Tradition and the Individual Talent" (1919), and his approval of the Agrarians—he had recently read *I'll Take My Stand*—gave support to a program that would have seemed deeply objectionable to Shapiro, even though the program found some of its sanctions in Jefferson's thought and Shapiro was, in some respects, a neo-Fugitive poet.[7]

"University" is in no direct sense a response to *After Strange Gods*, but to turn from the poem to the book is to discover an antagonism, however implicit, of ideologies. "What I mean by tradition," Eliot writes, "involves all those habitual actions, habits and customs, from the most significant religious rite to our conventional way of greeting a stranger, which represent the blood kinship of 'the same people living in the same place'" (18). (Compare Shapiro's "Equals shake hands, unequals blankly pass.") Similarly, to turn from Eliot's prose to Austen's descriptions of Donwell Abbey and the Abbey-Mill farm, is to discover an agreeement, however implicit, of ideologies. Donwell Abbey, we remember, is "the residence of a family of such true gentility, untainted in blood and understanding." The habitual actions and conventional greetings that separate Eliot and Shapiro as "unequals" unite Eliot and Austen as "equals"; questions of manners and manors, but also of blood and kinship, are at stake.

What then of Donwell Abbey: should our reading of Shapiro's poem alter our interpretation of Jane Austen's great good place? If it were to do so, there would be an irony to observe, for what we should be arguing would resemble Eliot's proposal in "Tradition and the Individual Talent" concerning the reflexive effect of the authentic modern work on traditional literary canons. A full answer to this question would require a discussion of a number of other questions. For example: is "University" an authentically modern work in Eliot's sense? As an innovative work, "University" yields to the other, more Audenesque and demotic poems that Delmore Schwartz admired in *Person, Place and Thing*. But there are other reasons for considering the nature of Eliot's influence on Shapiro. When Shapiro discusses the relation of poetry to belief in *Younger Son*, he refers approvingly to Keats's ideas of negative capability and of the poet who has no ethical or political character but "lives in gusto, be it foul or fair" (138). At the same time, he tacitly refers to Eliot's idea of poetic impersonality when (referring to himself in the third person) he describes the historical context in which "University" was written:

Today he knew that in his world the foul predominates, and there was no help for that except somehow to make the foul fair, make the poem a thing of beauty no matter what the ingredients. His was a time when the conflict of emotions waged war in the heart and mind, and the poem could hold the foul ingredients in suspension until the work emerged whole. All that was left was the dignity of the poem . . . and even the unworthiness of one's own feelings and sensations could be transmuted into a vision, however dark. (138-139)

Despite the strong echoes here of "Tradition and the Individual Talent," one may doubt whether the poem meets Eliot's ideal of poetic impersonality. The man who suffers and the poet who creates are *not* separate in "University," nor would one wish them to be. Indeed, one way of measuring the value of the poem is to recognize the force of Shapiro's attack on prejudice; and one way of doing this is to return to *Emma*, as an instance of "tradition," and to read (or re-read) it in the light of Shapiro's individual talent. Does *Emma* still succeed in promoting traditional values through the description of an ideal place? What Shapiro's subversive description of the university invites us to see—or to see more clearly, since it can be argued that the novel has this insight within it also [8] —is the class basis of Jane Austen's principles and the exclusionary implications of an "English" currency of values.

In *Emma* Jane Austen's "English" principles are threatened in two ways. They are threatened, first, by the secret behavior of Frank Churchill, the young man born in the Highbury community but adopted and brought up by an aristocratic family in Yorkshire. According to Mr. Knightley, Frank has "no *English* delicacy towards the feelings of other people" (emphasis added): "No, Emma [he says], your amiable young man can be amiable only in French, not in English. He may be very 'aimable,' have very good manners and be very agreeable; but he can have no English delicacy towards the feelings of other people: nothing really amiable about him" (149). Churchill's threat is the threat posed by an "equal" who fails to live up to the obligations of his position, most obviously in his secret engagement to Jane Fairfax. English values are threatened secondly by Mrs. Elton, nee Augusta Hawkins of Bristol, the heiress with L10,000, made in trade, who marries the Highbury vicar after Emma angrily rejects his proposal. If Frank Churchill knows the social rules but fails to obey them, she doesn't seem to know the rules in the first place. Addressing Mr. Knightley as "Knightley" and Miss Fairfax as "Jane," she assumes a familiarity obnoxious to the natives of Highbury; in the use of English names her currency is false. Calling her husband Mr. E. or her *caro sposo*, she is vulgar and pretentious by turns. Against her nouveau riche vulgarity Jane Austen sets Mr. Knightley's breeding. When Mrs. Elton claims that under her management everything will be "as natural and simple as possible" during the strawberry party, Knightley replies: "My idea of the simple and the natural will be to have the table spread in the dining-room. The nature and the simplicity of gentlemen and ladies, with their servants and furniture, I think is best observed by meals within doors. When you are tired of eating strawberries in the garden, there shall be cold meat in the house" (355). A magnificent putdown, of course, and one which Trilling, an American Jewish writer with different cultural commitments than Shapiro, did not find exceptionable. With Shapiro's poem in mind, however, are we not made aware of the ideological character of Knightley's values—of how his "English" principles are partly a function of his xenophobia, and of how his definition of what is "natural" defends, and derives from, a specific set of class practices? We need not doubt the sincerity of Jane Austen's belief that nature and culture are complementary terms, or that manners, when informed by morals, are the very stuff of civilized life; but with "University" before us, we are likely to resist the temptation to erect her values into a set of universal principles. As Shapiro sees them in "University," manners are one means whereby traditional power maintains its hegemony. And when at the end of *Emma* the heroine—with her fortune of L30,000, marries Mr. Knightley, scion of a family of true gentility, "untainted in blood and understanding," what is this but an example of "equals" shaking hands? It would be difficult, but it might be possible—at least as an exercise—to rewrite the scene of the strawberry party from Mrs. Elton's point of view—to see her, like the young poet in Charlottesville, as undergoing a trial by culture, an ordeal of civility, and as responding just as abrasively to the "nonsense of the gracious lawn."[9]

NOTES

[1] For a consideration of the "disconcerting" effect of these sentences, see Reino, 85.

[2] Tate's phrase is from "Letter to a Poet," in *Common Sense* (February 1943); cited in Reino, 23.

[3] For an amusing deflation of Yeats, see Shapiro's "W.B.Y." in *Collected Poems: 1940-1978* (280); the deflation is the more pointed in that it immediately precedes a tribute to "W.H.A."

[4] On a larger scale is Carter's Grove on the James river; on a smaller scale is Appomattox Manor. The Virginia manor house provides, of course, an important link with English culture, several being names after places in England (e.g., Brandon, Bromton, Wilton, Stratford), as Calder Loth points out in his prefatory note to Gleason's volume.

[5] Before its reprinting in *Beyond Culture*, Trilling's essay had appeared earlier on both sides of the Atlantic: as an introduction to the Riverside edition of *Emma* (Boston: Houghton Mifflin, 1957), and as an article with the title "Emma" in *Encounter*, 8 (June 1957): 49-59.

[6] This assumption has been confirmed by Mr. Shapiro, who is not sure when exactly he first read Eliot's work (personal communication).

[7] Reino, 157-59.

[8] Despite the values Jane Austen accords to Donwell Abbey, the novel shows, perhaps unintentionally, that the older law of the

manor is not equipped to deal with Jane Fairfax, the woman of talent but no money, whose place in English society is marginal and precarious.

[9] I wish to express my deep thanks to Rick Chess for his invaluable help. I am also thankful to the following who kindly read and helpfully commented on drafts of this essay: Dan Cottom, Melvyn New, Beth Schwartz, Virginia Seacrist, John Frederick Nims. More generally, I am indebted to constructive comments made by members of the Faculty / Student Forum at the University of South Florida and of the Cardiff Critical Seminar at the University of Wales.

Works Cited

Austen, Jane. *Emma*. Ed. R. W. Chapman, New York: Oxford University Press, 1982.

Barthes, Roland. *Mythologies*. Trans. Annette Lavers. New York: Hill and Wang, 1972.

Cowley, Malcolm. *Exile's Return*. New York: Norton, 1934.

Eliot, T. A. *After Strange Gods: A Primer of Modern Heresy*. New York: Harcourt, Brace, 1934.

_____. "Tradition and the Individual Talent." *The Egoist* 6 (September/October, November/December, 1919): 54-55, 72-73.

Gleason, David King. *Virginia Plantation Homes*. Baton Rouge: Lousiana State University Press, 1989.

James, Henry. *English Hours*. New York: Weidenfeld and Nicolson, 1989.

Reino, Joseph. *Karl Shapiro*. Boston: Twayne, 1981.

Schwartz, Delmore. "The Poet's Progress." *The Nation* 156.2 (January 9, 1943): 63-64.

Shapiro, Karl. *Collected Poems 1940-1978*. New York: Random House,1978.

——————. *The Bourgeois Poet*. New York: Random House, 1964.

——————. *In Defense of Ignorance*. New York: Random House, 1960.

——————. "The Jewish Writer and the English Literary Tradition." *Commentary* 8 (1949): 369-70.

——————. *Person, Place and Thing*. New York: Reynal and Hitchcock, 1942.

——————. *Poems of a Jew*. New York: Random House, 1958.

——————. *The Younger Son*. Chapel Hill. N.C.: Algonquin Books, 1988.

Trilling, Lionel. *E. M. Forster*. New York: New Directions, 1943.

——————. "*Emma* and the Legend of Jane Austen." *Beyond Culture*. New York: Viking Press, 1968. 31-55.

Yeats, William. Butler. *Collected Poems*. New York: Macmillan, 1956.

~ 𝒦𝒮 ~
Leo Haber
ABOUT KARL SHAPIRO

(sh-p-r: [Hebrew verb root, transitive, piel construction that is more emphatic] to beautify, to improve something else, not oneself)

>He scorned gardens of the mind
garlanded with papier-mâché flowers
of flaming red and gorgeous yellow
and *chalooshis* purple that would draw
the crowd of hoary horticulturists

>primed to scamper after every blatant
burgeoning of false Van Goghian color.
He nurtured homegrown and eastern plants
wavering in the west wind—fine,
fragile petals in muted shades that spread

>their souls to no pounding hordes and
sought the sun in the shade of great oaks
and busy bees and poisonous snakes curling
to strike. In the Talmudic phrase,
"*Kishmo, ken hoo*," "Like his name, so is he,"

>a beautifyer, an improver, a patient
cherisher of all that is good, lovely,
honest, and true, but also redolent of
times past and of sweet scents to come
down the long shaped row heading toward the distant

>but marvelous moment of redemption.

Note: *chalooshis*: Yiddish word for grossly ugly to the point of causing one to faint. The initial "ch" is pronounced as in "Bach."

~ *KS* ~

Joseph Harris

THE TOWING OF THE POETRY WRECK

Alas, Mr. Shapiro As pilot of The Poetry Wreck, You've sailed dangerous waters With your American ballast Of dead poets and those almost alive. Like the Flying Dutchman, You've found no friendly shore To moor your craft, and for Your sin against the American Dream You're doomed to anchor at no port.

Prophet or propagandist? You've opened poetry's Pandora's Box, And loosed the killers of the dream. The Poetic muse is on the run, Safe no more where it long has Slept under democracy's wing. You would have it that even Whitman, Our one true poet of democracy, Wrote only prose, and that poetry's Too autocratic an art to flourish here.

Alas, Mr. Shapiro, Do you not see dimly Somewhere off the American shore, A poet at the helm of his unseen craft, Signaling even now, ready to tow Your wandering Poetry Wreck to land?

~ 𝒦𝒮 ~
Ted Kooser
KARL SHAPIRO IN THE EARLY SIXTIES

In late summer, 1963, my first wife and I packed up our clothing, our few sticks of second-hand furniture, our wedding gifts and our courage and lumbered westward on balding tires. Both of us had been brought up in Iowa, and neither of us had ever lived more than an hour's drive from home. I was crazy with fear but too vain to admit that to my wife, who set her broad Danish forehead into the winds of uncertainty, found a high school teaching job near Lincoln, Nebraska, settled us into an apartment, and began to plan for the future.

I had been admitted to the University of Nebraska as a graduate student in English, but I had little interest in a scholarly career. I was an aspiring poet, and had applied to Nebraska because Karl Shapiro was teaching there. I had read Karl's books and knew that he was among the two or three most important poets of his generation. I wanted to throw myself at his feet.

I enrolled in two of Karl's classes, a writing class and a lecture on contemporary poetry. By the end of the first semester he and I had become friends. He was then fifty years old, wiry and energetic, witty and charming. He had a slight lisp, an imperfection that I imagined he had compensated for by teaching himself to write beautifully. I remember wondering if perhaps I ought to try to develop a small flaw that I too could write my way out and around, not recognizing that I already was possessed by enough demons to keep me in poems for the rest of my life.

What I most clearly remember about Karl during that period were his eyes, bright and alert behind heavy glasses that magnified their size. He had a bemused, sidewise, almost birdlike glance that he reserved for occasions when someone said something stupid—a glance that I often saw during the pontifications one suffers through at English Department parties.

Karl was then writing the cranky and explosive prose poems of *The Bourgeois Poet*, works whose form was dictated, he said, by the size and shape of a regular sheet of typing paper. They were the first prose poems

I had ever read. I could feel the heat rolling off those manuscript pages. I was then living among the things and people that he was transforming into poems and it was a thrilling experience for a young writer. His beautiful daughter, Kathy, who was at the center of some of the poems, was my good friend. I came to know his wife and his other children. At his home he had a coffee table made from a slate blackboard upon which he wrote with sticks of colored chalk. I recall looking at the merest of his doodles with a kind of reverence. I worshipped the dust of his erasures.

Though the regular professorial staff was skeptical, Karl was a well-prepared lecturer and a kind and thoughtful teacher of writing. I was completely devoted to him. By the following spring I had so neglected my required academic work and so given myself to the reading and writing of poetry that my advisor called me into his office. He gathered his face around the gravity of its errand, touched the tips of his fingers together—once, twice, three times—and announced that the department would not renew my financial assistance for the following year. I had, after all, neglected my coursework and had spent far too much time with…well, you know who. It hadn't been necessary to mention Karl's name; the message was clear.

This happened during the dark ages before Creative Writing. It was a time when English professors with legitimate Ph.Ds were dreadfully uneasy about the presence among them of poets and fiction writers. Though Karl's international reputation, his past editorship of *Poetry*, and his Pulitzer prize commanded a good deal of respect, he had been assigned a small office down the hall and around a corner, where it was unlikely that serious graduate students would be touched by the siren song of creative writing that whistled out of his keyhole.

I was young and naive, and I had never expected to be booted out of the graduate program. I had no idea what I was going to do with the rest of my life. When I talked to Karl about what had happened, he counselled me that if I really wanted to be a writer I ought to get a regular eight-to-five job, something completely divorced from scholarly work. I took that advice. By mid-summer, 1964, I was working as a clerk at a life insurance company, and I have continued in that line of work during the intervening years. I saw Karl frequently, and on Saturdays and Sundays we often took long drives through the country in my deeply-mortgaged new convertible, taking the summer sun and drinking beer in the country bars. In the second volume of Karl's autobiography, *Reports of My Death*, there is a photograph of us on one of those outings. In that picture I look as happy as I have ever looked.

In those days, Lincoln was a smaller town than it is today. The Lincoln newspapers had gushy social features, describing the clothing and bridge parties and culinary delights of the country-club set. This practice had hung on from the 19th century, when William Jennings Bryan dined with Lincoln's finest and everyone in Nebraska wanted to know if he broke wind. In one full half-page spread was a photo of Karl and his wife with another couple: "Mr. and Mrs. Gotrocks entertain Pulitzer Prize Winning Poet and Spouse" read the cutline. Karl told me later that he had been invited to dinner and had had no idea that the press had been asked to send a camera man. It was embarrassments like this, I'm certain, that inspired some of the spleen Karl was later to spew on Lincoln society in his novel, *Edsel*.

In the spring of 1965, Allen Ginsberg, Peter and Julius Orlovsky and a pair of cup-bearers whose names I've forgotten came to Lincoln at the unofficial invitation of a student. They were crossing the country in an old VW microbus and came up from Kansas, where Allen had begun his poem "Wichita Vortex Sutra." Ginsberg and Peter Orlovsky visited English classes at the University of Nebraska, read outrageous gay poetry, embarrassed the farm boys, horrified the farm girls, and generally disrupted most of eastern Nebraska. The professorial staff gathered in clusters, chirping like quail.

Karl made himself scarce during the day, but that evening joined up with Ginsberg's entourage at a party in an old house near campus. Karl seemed stiff and cautious, Allen was chanting and tinkling his finger-cymbals. With the two of them there, those in the house that evening experienced the highest concentration of important poets Lincoln has ever known. During that same visit, Ginsberg made a little drawing on the wall of the bathroom at Karl's apartment, and the landlords faithfully preserved this icon for many years.

I recall that T. S. Eliot died at about that time. Karl had attacked Eliot and his followers and there was little love lost between them. During a locally produced television show, a professor showed a photo taken in the offices of *Poetry* some years before in which Karl and Eliot were chatting. The professor, apparently trying to put Karl in a subordinate position to the revered Eliot, said, "Here is Karl Shapiro asking Mr. Eliot a question. Just what was the answer, Karl?" To which Karl snapped, "Frankly, I don't even remember asking a question."

On the day Eliot died, I walked into Karl's office and he was sitting with his feet up on the radiator, looking out across the parking lot. He had a bemused look on his face. He told me that he had just received a phone call from Caroline Gordon, who had said, with exaggerated sentiment, "Karl, *Tom* is dead."

One day, as I was standing in the door to his office visiting with him, a look of nameless horror came over his face. He was looking into space over my shoulder, his eyes wide and terrified. I first thought that he was having some sort of a seizure, and I thought, "My God, the famous poet, Karl Shapiro, is having a seizure and it will be up to me to help him through it!" Then I immediately realized what was happening. A starling had somehow made its way into the building and was making a bee-line down the hallway straight for Karl's head. He had seen it over my shoulder as it came flapping toward him. Up he jumped, ducking and bobbing, and out the door he went, slamming the door behind him and locking me in the office with the bird, who flew around and around, then slammed into the wall and fell behind a bookcase full of poetry, dead as a stone.

Karl left Lincoln forever in mid-1965. He had accepted a teaching position at the Chicago circle campus of the University of Illinois. In his wake, the pages of *Edsel* sifted down upon Lincoln like a flock of buzzards. Karl was never forgiven for what was considered to be his mean-spirited, vicious attack on Lincoln, its university, and its people. It was quite a funny book, really. Several years ago, I asked one of the senior faculty members why Karl had never been invited back to read his poems. I was told with a haughty sniff, "We never thought that he would *want* to come." Ah, yes.

~ KS ~

J.T. Ledbetter

SHAPIRO: THREE MEMORIES

It was a warm Nebraska afternoon and when you walked in with Stephen Spender we knew what you wanted: response!

But we sat and listened to the man with the pipe, elbow-patches tweed coat and resonant voice and asked, said, nothing: no response.

As time wore on (as Augustine says time is wont to do) and Shapiro shifted uneasily next to the great man and scowled at us. Each of us waited for another to raise the hand, ask the question, comment on something. Anything!

I think it was the way Spender looked wistfully out the window when it was mercifully done that did it for me. All of us followed his look out the window at the great Nebraska sky, trying not to look at Shapiro, thinking continually of those ...

II

"My secretary left." We waited for the other shoe to drop. Nothing. Then, "She left to get married." Silence. Finally: "She took the grade book for this class with her ..."

III

When I got to the U that morning I found him alone in his office and told him I'd heard that his friend Randall Jarrell had been killed. He looked at me for a very long time then turned to the window and stared out toward the library, a few trees bending in the forever wind, and he put his hand to his head in a way I still remember but still can't describe and said ... I can't remember what he said. He just stood there watching the trees whip back and forth in the wind and the students walking to the library, their bags and bright scarves bits of blown color beneath the lowering sky.

~*KS*~

Glenna Luschei

ORIGINALS

Well, Karl. We can't believe it now,
but I used to be
your secretary. When *Howl*

came out you sent congratulations
to Ginsberg.
I took your calm

dictation in my impeccable
Gregg's shorthand
then heisted the letter home

for my army clerk husband
to type. I presented the originals
& carbons to you at 9:00 a.m.

clean as a new baby. You said "Ahem.
Good work." You, handsome
with your white hair, a real poet!

Luckily
I soon had a new baby. You sent me
congratulations.

When I came back you had a real
secretary. You looked guilty.
I cried. You said,

"*Howl* will change our lives."

~ _KS_ ~

Glenna Luschei

MACHINE

Alexander Wat, futurist
wrote the way a snake curled
in a jar would write.

I dissipate my poems like smoke
from a machine stalled dead
center.

Let me write
like the galloping hooves of the
Arab horse.

Alexander, you were in prison
when you had that vision of Satan
with hooves.
I have been stampeded.

We embrace—you the strange politics;
I, distraction.

You heard anti-aircraft fire
as the Devil's laughter.

I see waste.
Chips of my life fly out of the hopper.

I return each year to Nebraska
where I studied with Karl Shapiro.
You returned to Poland.

Who can say that hell
comes only from bodily torture?

I, too, study
the nature of evil.

Glenna Luschei

GIRAFFE OR SCHOLARS

Once I submitted
to you at *Prairie Schooner*,
a poem starting
with the line from Rimbaud:
"Back from hot lands"

I'm "back from hot lands"
Where grass grew up to my collar
and I'm a giraffe
back to my scholars.

How have I breezed in?
Am I the mane of the wind?

You know, a student poem.

I waited.

Waited.

Berg and Mezey
heard from you.

Finally
I asked my army clerk husband.
He forked over the letter,
opened.

A rejection!

Mailed six weeks earlier.

Written in your hand, "Send more poems."

Sorry, Karl,
for waiting thirty years.
Hope it's not too late.

~ KS ~
Jim Lynch
KARL SHAPIRO: SIX DECADES OF PER-VERSE

A gorilla lives in the basement of Karl Shapiro's poetry. Usually, he is a cranial and playful gorilla, but a gorilla nevertheless, with all that "gorilla" implies: primitive strength, sudden ferocity, willful aloofness. To be sure, the major strands of Shapiro's poetry—the urbanity, the humor, the cleverness—deserve major attention, and these elements coincide more clearly with Shapiro's civilized demeanor. But his fierceness runs like an undercurrent through his poems; the current snags on some hidden rock and the whirlpool poem forms.

From a poem entitled "The Glutton" in the 1942 collection, *Person, Place, and Thing,* a young Shapiro writes:

> I am glad that his stomach will eat him away in revenge,
> Digesting itself when his blubber is lain in the earth.
> Let the juice of his gluttony swallow him inward like lime
> And leave of his volume only the mould of his girth.

Or in another early poem, this one called "Nigger" from the V-Letter collection of 1944:

> When you felt that loop and you took that boot from a KKK,
> And your hands hung down and your face went out in a blast of grape,
> Did the Lord say yes, did the Lord say no … ?
> Are you coming to peace, O Booker T. Lincoln Roosevelt Jones,
> And is Jesus riding to raise your wage and cut that cord?

This strand of ferocity moves right through to the eighties in poems like "Girls Fighting, Broadway":

> a scream retches into the traffic
> they are down
> on the polluted sidewalk clawing and ripping
> and hurling fuck

And even in a seemingly sedate poem like "Human Nature" (1973):

> For months and years in a forgotten war
> I rode the battle-gray Diesel-stinking ships
> Among the brilliantly advertised Pacific Islands
> Coasting the sinister New Guinea coasts,
> All during the killing and hating of a forgotten war.
> Now when I drive behind a Diesel-stinking bus
> On the way to the university to teach
> Stevens and Pound and Mallarmé
> I am homesick for war.

Within the mild and gentlemanly poet, within the courteous civilized person, a witches' brew of contempt, disgust, and scorn that withers its object boils. One gets the feeling that writing a poem like "The Intellectual" was for the poet an act similar to scraping plaque from teeth:

> Do something! Die in Spain ...
> or go into business
> Or start another little magazine
> Move in with a woman or have a kid
> I'd rather be a barber and cut hair
> Than walk with you in museum halls.
> You, l'homme qui rit,
> Swallow your stale saliva.

Wastrels have been the butt of satire from the time of Horace and before, but Shapiro's contempt for the smugly unproductive—"Pothead, show me your book!"—rivals the most stinging depictions.

In a review of Arthur Miller's autobiography, *Timebends*, Alfred Kazin said that what he liked most about the book was "the irrepressible vehemence," the "honest sense of disaffection." One might appreciate Shapiro's poetry for the same reasons. But what is it, specifically, for Shapiro, that elicits the vehement poem, the gorilla-like, spontaneous ferocity?

The merging of Hollywood and Washington, D.C., the pretentiousness of much modern poetry, and the succumbing of the American public to PR seem to call out the fiercest feeling. Cumulatively, these add up to a protest against the uglification of America—Shapiro hates the ugly speech of a people inhabiting an ugly landscape and who are infatuated with ugly Hollywood and TV images.

In Norman Rockwell's famous portrait of a drug-store, we view the solicitous clerk, spotless cap of soda-jerk, leaning over the gleaming chrome, accommodating, with the heaping ice-cream soda, the happy urchin-cum-dog. In Shapiro's "Drugstore"

> every nook and cranny of the flesh
> Is spoken to by packages with wiles.
> "Buy me, buy me," they whimper and cajole;
> The hectic range of lipstick pouts,
> Revealing the wicked and the simple mouth ...
> Crude fellowships are made and lost;
> They slump in booths like rags not even drunk.

Though not intoxicated, these fellows who slump in booths have drunken hearts, full of desire for what is crass and common. In Norman Rockwell streets, cozy diners and kids on bikes; the streets of Shapiro's "Israfel" are crowded with "pawnshops, and whores, and sour little bars." The dwellers in row houses lead row lives:

> Glass after glass, door after door the same,
> Face after face, the same, the same,
> The brutal visibility the same ...
> All day from porch to porch they weave
> A nonsense pattern through the even glare,
> Stealing in surfaces
> Cold vulgar glances at themselves.
>   "The Dome of Sunday"

And when they are not in their ugly row houses, nor visiting their gaudy drugstores, nor their gaudy drugged whores, they are in bars with "murals of lust, movies for men" and,

> A waxworks of syphilitics; shooting range,
> Phrenologist and tattoo artist: all
>   Quacks who apprehend
>   And speak the dirty word.
>   "Honkytonk"

The dive is an important image for Shapiro; it crystallizes the ugliness of a once pretty landscape. How much of America is represented by the dive? How far does it extend as an image of the country? What has it not contaminated? "Washington Cathedral" is full of "fake magnificence." At the Lincoln Memorial one views the great man "whittled to a fool's colossus." In "D.C." people

> live with an easy homelessness
> And common tastelessness, their souls
> Weakly lit up by blazing screens and tales
> Told by a newspaper.

In "Hollywood,"

> the bodyguard,
> The parasite, the scholar are well paid,
> The quack erects his alabaster office
> The moron and the genius are enshrined....
> And beauty is marketed like a basic food.

Hollywood has reached D.C., coast to coast a huge "Necropolis" where men "bring home hate like evening papers." The gorilla in Karl Shapiro would like to smash the heads of the image-mongers who have sold size for magnificence, height for loftiness, deliberate speech for wisdom. The heart is drunk on banality.

In the schools: dry intellectuals, commercial deans, gangster students—and this is where the banal go to escape from their banality.

> In side streets the coming generation waits its turn. Their hero is still in high school. He drives a hundred miles an hour into a tree.
> "The look of shock" *The Bourgeois Poet*

Criminal youngsters age cynically and go off to the "University" where

> The Deans, dry spinsters over family plate ...
> Humor the snob and lure the lout.
> Within the precincts of this world

> Poise is a club....
> The school takes from the nobleman his name,
> Falls open like a dishonest look
> And shows us, rotted and endowed,
> its senile pleasure.

It is a benefit that "exams flush everything out of their minds" ("The History of Philosophy Professor"). This newly educated gangster carries his values with him all through college and comes out on the other side with those values intact, the new barbarian who "knows nothing, doesn't care that he knows nothing, and tells you so" (*To Abolish Children*). His sullen defiance and latent banality have turned to swagger. His standards elicit furious mockery:

> Be natural as an American abroad who knows no language, not even American. Learn how to walk the way you want. Slump your shoulders, stick your belly out, arms all over the table.
> "Lower the standard"

Wherever one looks, one finds the gaudy-ugly, the huckster, the deluded, the incompetent. In the hospital,

> how I slept! and woke to your hard professional slaps in
> the face, in Recovery, nurse. You must have been late for
> your date, good-looking nurse; your make-up was perfect
> when I saw you at last.
> "Little tendon" *The Bourgeois Poet*

On television news, the banal are suckered by the sellers:

> The General returns with the power of a god. His disgrace is his triumph. The world pours at his feet like a tide ... The General is handsome, arrogant, and wrong. Such a General might be President. He delivers his profile to rich and poor.
> "After the war"

And in his own beloved discipline,

> There is a hell, the hell of sick poets ....
> Those who mistake rage for intensity, symmetry

or design, metaphor for focus, drunkenness for vision.
"As richly documented"
On the occasion of the death of a political
party, I send an epitaph by Western Union.
I didn't go to the funeral of poetry. I stayed
home and watched it on television.
"The password of the 20th century"

Does this make Shapiro sound like the Thersites of American verse, or does it seem self-evident that poets will occasionally express furious feelings? One must remember, first, the selectiveness of the quotations. More importantly, one must remember that Shapiro knew a different time—before commercialized intellectualism, before the endless exposures of idiots and cheats in high office, before a walk on the upper West Side of Manhattan was dangerous, before K-Mart, before McDonalds, before soap operas, and before TV; before a time when girls fought without shame on Broadway in front of an aroused and approving crowd, before "Friday the 13th, Part whatever," before Rod McKuen was a popular poet in America, before students became known for their insolence and before courtesy became a virtue for nerds; before Pat Robertson could become a bonafide presidential candidate, before the blossoming junkyard on the outskirts of every town, before what is ugly and common and cheap and bland became acceptable and even sought after. It must be anger-producing to witness this oppressive levelling—Donald Trump's *The Art of the Deal* a number one best-seller! The wonder is that so few serious poets do not seem to be incarnations of Thersites. A sentient creature living in a degenerating milieu will react more fiercely than someone oblivious to the degeneration. The ferocity in Shapiro's poetry signals a scarred psyche, a psyche that has observed and lived through substantial decay. Though he has responded to this decay with clenched teeth, Shapiro has managed to keep his gorilla in the basement.

In 1969 Shapiro gave a poetry reading with Louis Simpson at UC Davis; a handful of faculty and about a dozen graduate students turned out. That same week UCD hosted a poetry reading by Richard Brautigan;

the largest auditorium on campus could not hold the student turnout—the reading was moved out to the quad.

How well Shapiro has managed to maintain his magnanimity and how well he has accommodated the fierce feeling is reflected by the following: before I wrote this paper, I told Shapiro that I was going to give a talk on him at a conference, but that all I had decided on at that point was that the first sentence would read, "A gorilla lives in the basement of Karl Shapiro's poetry." He wrote to me:

> When I lived in Chicago I was close by the Lincoln Park Zoo and visited Sinbad the gorilla 2 or 3 times a week. I had such admiration for this animal, his eyes and his grooming (every hair immaculately in place) and his expressive boredom. I think he liked me. When I stood in front of the cage he would look at me a while and then slap the hanging tire with the back of his hand without looking. I would nod to him. I should have written an elegy when he died but missed the opportunity. Is he the one in my basement?

~ *KS* ~

James E. Miller, Jr.

KARL SHAPIRO IN NEBRASKA

I first met Karl Shapiro when he came to Lincoln, Nebraska, in 1956, to edit the Prairie Schooner and to teach creative writing. As chairman of the Department of English, I hired him. That year he was forty-three and I was thirty-six; but I remember both of us as young, the future as wide open as the empty prairies around us. We had both been in the army during World War II, but he had been a medic in the Pacific and had seen the war, I had been a code-breaker in Intelligence on the Potomac and had seen Washington, D.C. When I think of that war, I find my memory dominated by the images Karl shaped in *V-Letter and Other Poems*, the book he published in 1944 and which won him the Pulitzer Prize while he was still in the Pacific somewhere: "Troop Train," "The Gun," "Sunday: New Guinea," "The Leg," "V-Letter," "Elegy for a Dead Soldier."

One of the things we discovered we shared was an admiration of Walt Whitman, who was generally out of favor at the time. My colleague Bernice Slote and I had combined efforts to write an essay relating Whitman to Dylan Thomas, then quite popular because of his scandalous lecture tours in America. The essay, published in 1959, was called "Of Monkeys, Nudes, and the Good Gray Poet." Karl that same year published "The first White Aboriginal," linking Whitman and D.H. Lawrence. The three of us decided to join forces showing the enduring vitality of Whitman as manifested in important contemporary writers. It seemed a daring enterprise, flying in the face of the dominant literary voices of the time, both poetic and critical. It was, in the academies, the era of Pound and Eliot and of a "new criticism" tailored to analyze their poems. Our manifesto-like book, issued in 1960, was given a title meant to startle: *Start with the Sun: Studies in Cosmic Poetry*. The first part of the title was from Lawrence, the second from Whitman, both poets scorned by the new criticism. My copy still has its dust-jacket, with a picture of Bernice, Karl and me on the back, all looking implausibly young and having a lively literary discussion.

It always comes as something of a surprise when I remember that Karl had published several book of poetry before *V-Letter*. And I recall how surprised critics were when, in Nebraska, this poet who had been hailed as leading a movement reintroducing traditional forms in American poetry, began to publish prose poems that would, in 1964, he brought together as a book entitled *The Bourgeois Poet*. Karl had given to me a clutch of these poems to publish in *College English*, which I edited at the time. I put them as the lead piece in the May, 1962 issue.

I have often thought that if Nebraska influenced Karl as a poet, that influence was to be found most easily in *The Bourgeois Poet*. He lived with his wife and three children in a ranch-style house in a suburb of Lincoln. He had a salaried job, classes to meet, bills to pay, income taxes to figure. In some ways Karl's book was a poetic reaction to the time and place, similar in spirit to two other books of that period: *The Organization Man* (1956) and *The Man in the Gray Flannel Suit* (1955). Everything surrounding Karl was Taming; he himself deep down was wild. Of course, Allen Ginsberg's *Howl* had appeared in 1956, introduced by William Carlos Williams, a poet Karl admired and who admired him. In *The Bourgeois Poet,* Karl seems to be in spirit one of the beats, yearning for the open road, but entrapped instead in academia and stranded somewhere on the Great Plains. Remember that this view is spun from my imagination many years after.

But of course Karl could never have been part of any movement for long: he was too much himself, an independent spirit. I have in fancy thought off and on of writing two essays I have not yet written (and probably never will). One is a sweeping critical essay covering the novels of Thomas Wolfe from *Look Homeward Angel* to *You Can't Go Home Again*, which would show how the books are one vast modern *self-reflective* epic which anticipates the post-modernist fiction distinguished by taking itself for its subject, by being about its own creation. The other is an essay on Karl's *The Bourgeois Poet,* which I would entitle "Walt's Open Road Leads to Nebraska," and in which I would begin with a close (but not new-critical) look at Number 34, opening: "I am an atheist who says his prayers, / I am an anarchist, and a full professor at that. I take the loyalty oath. / I am a deviate. I fondle and contribute, backscuttle and brown, father of three." This section runs from pages 34 to 47 (note: 13 pages!), and a portion of it included in Karl's *Collected Poems: 1940-1978* (1978) is given the revealing title "Nebraska." It opens, "I love Nowhere where the factories die of malnutrition", the spirit of the sixteen-line excerpt is caught in the following three lines, which carry over the "I love Nowhere where" introduced at the beginning:

Where every tree is planted by hand and has a private tutor.
Where the "Parts" have to be ordered and the sky settles all questions,
Where travelers from California bitch at the backwardness and New Yorkers step on the gas in a panic...

Of course, Karl did not get Nebraska out of his system with *the Bourgeois Poet*. It was the locale and in some sense the subject of his novel, *Edsel* (1971). And it figures as it must in his second autobiographical volume, *Reports of My Death* (1990). Clearly Nebraska left its stamp on his imagination. Its vast skies, lonely trees, distant horizons, and scrubby sandhills do have lasting effect. I left in 1962 and still see it often in my dreams; Karl left in 1966 and I am sure it still lurks in his psyche. We continue to share Nebraska.

~KS~

John F. Nims

SPONTANEOUS EFFUSION IN HONOR OF KARL SHAPIRO

At his reading at the University of Illinois at Chicago, December 1965

Hail bard! we begin; this here being in noble diction, sublime-type.
 All two-bit words; skip the dime-type!
High encomium this, in an age little prone to the encomiastic:
You say, "One encomium please." and the clerk says "Just got 'em in plastic."
Karl Shapiro comes to us today; a bard, he, far-famed and distinguished,
To appreciate which it's enough to know English good and not be no linguisht,
Because practically every-kind book on Amer. Lit. (Contemp.)
Features Karl Shapiro prominently, and that is a real fact and not something I dremp.
Now, by birth Karl Shapiro comes to us from the historic South, all da more
Since he was born not just in Maryland but in its state capital which is (I hope)—oh you know.
His first book was published when he was off campaigning in the South Pacific,
And a Partisan Review said its prosodic modalities were dynamized O.K., and everybody else said, Hey terrific!
Its name was called *Person, Place AND Thing*,
Thay, it thet the thoul danthing!
(That's lisping in numbers, like Pope said.) Anyway, when the poet was still engaged with the Japanese, and I don't mean on a fourteen-mile haiku,

Far from home, missing the good American things, the malts and
    the bingo and the chocolate-covered graham craiku,
His next book appeared, *V-Letter and Other Poems,*
You know 'ems?
For which he was awarded, among sundry prizes, the Pulitzer.
Now some prizes are lallapaloosas, but others are even
    lallapaloolitzer;
And this one is the lallapaloolitzist, next to the pealing of
    the Nobel,
Whose tintinnabulations, as one of them Baltimore bards said,
    do so musically swell.
And which of Karl Shapiro's honors ought to be probably the next,
At least if this prize is on the level and not as it sometimes
    is, fexed.
(And if anybody wonders why the Nobel has such kudos,
It's because of some prizes there is many, but of Nobels, man,
    dey is few dose!)
Still in the South Pacific, and with no reference libraries at hand,
    but only with his memory to serve for numerous allusions,
    quotations, etc., he summed up all poetry and especially
    metrics in his *Essay on Rime.*
Among whose admirers of, I'm.
Next book, *Trial of a Poet;*
If you haven't read it, then do, on account of to yourself y'owe it.
Then we have a great book, *Poems One Nine Four O-One Nine Five
    Eleven*;
Well, *One Nine Five Three*, really, but that's harder for me
    to rime than for you to subtract, sort of, seven.
Five years later, to show he was still around and hadn't bade
    the Muse "Cheerio!"
Karl Shapiro's next book was *Poems of a Jew* by Karl Shapeerio.
Cognizance should now be took of a collection of essays called by
    name *In Defense of Ignorance*;
And if you think I can't think of a rime for "ignorance," well,

you're entitled to your own opinion.
Which if maybe it—the book—had no poetry in it, it did put
    the *verse* in controversial
And cut a wide swath with good gleaning there. "By the peck, hey?"
    No, by the burshel.
And then just last year there came *The Poet (Bourgeois)*
Which welled up from some deep atavistic chthonic joy, or, as
    we intellectuals say, Man, that crazy *Ur*-joie!
He also wrote *Idylls of the King, Little Women,* and *The Wake
    of Finnegan*
"Oh go on; he didn't either!" He did so, by poetic license, this
    being the one line I may never have the chance to rime in again.
At last, end of encomium,
(To which if there's objections you got please forgo me 'em)
Saying only to Karl in conclusion
And availing myself of an apt lit. allusion:
In the garden of the Muses eine ritzy Blume du bist,
Being not only the Karl that is Shapiro but also the one that
    is Shapirior and Shapiriest.

~*KS*~

John Frederick Nims

THE EARLY YEARS

Karl Shapiro's work and career are too rich and various for me to hope to encompass here. My remarks confine themselves to those early poems, which surprised and delighted me then and which continue to hold my admiration and affection. My discussion of them will be based largely on my first reactions to the poetry as I recorded them at the time.

During the summer of 1940 I was on the campus of the University of Chicago, for the most part pleasantly engaged with classes in Greek and French tragedy. But I had been writing verse too, and when I heard that George Dillon, then editor of POETRY, was to offer a course on the contemporary poets, I readily made room for it on my schedule. Hadn't he won the Pulitzer Prize eight years before, and didn't I remember with pleasure such lines of his as

> ... though nevermore from Spain
> The little ships with laughter in their wake
> Will sail to the Americas again ...

and hadn't he translated Baudelaire with Millay, whose passionately liberated lyrics had been among my high-school favorites?

Tall, dignified, but witty and genial in discussion, he shared with us his inside knowledge of the craft he knew so well; it was the first time I had the chance to hear a real poet talk about real poetry.

My single most vivid memory of his sessions was of the day when, always ready to share his enthusiasms with us, he brought into class a manuscript he had just received at the magazine. That afternoon we in the class became among the earliest admirers of the young writer, a then unknown Karl J. Shapiro of Baltimore. The poem Dillon brought to us was not at all like his own work; it was a mark of his taste and generosity as editor that he was open to excellence of many kinds. As he read the poem, and then talked about it, I was struck by the directness and strength of the diction, the aptness of the imagery, and the liberties the poet took with a familiar rhythm. The poem was "Necropolis."

EVEN in death they prosper, even in the death
Where lust lies senseless and pride fallow
The moldering owners of rents and labor
Prosper and improve the high hill.

For theirs is the stone whose name is deepest cut;
Theirs the facsimile temple, theirs
The iron acanthus and the hackneyed Latin,
The boxwood rows and all the birds.

And even in death the poor are thickly herded
In intimate congestion under streets and alleys.
Look at the standard sculpture, the cheap
Synonymous slabs, the machined crosses.

Yes, even in death the cities are unplanned.
The heirs govern from the marble centers;
They will not remove. And the ludicrous angels,
Remains of the poor, will never fly
But only multiply in the green grass.

Dillon must already have sent his letter of acceptance. Shapiro, in his autobiographical *The Younger Son*, describes the "day in August" when it reached him:

> He could see the yellow trolley floating toward him several blocks away as he tore open the small envelope printed simply *Poetry* and which he assumed was an ad. Inside was a blue slip with a letterhead, a rather pre-Raphaelite Pegasus, and the name and address of the Chicago magazine. His eye lighted on the words, "We are pleased to accept for publication," and listed four of his poems. The streetcar stopped for him and opened its door with a welcoming sigh, but the poet waved to the conductor, and turned and ran back to his apartment. He called the store and said he could not come in that day. Then he sat back and read holes in the blue notice, and went and got the poems they had accepted and studied them with new eyes.

But not so new as his readers' eyes would have been when, a few weeks after we had heard the poem with new ears, it was published in POETRY. With it were three others, including "University," with its challenging first lines:

> To hurt the Negro and avoid the Jew
> Was the curriculum ...

Two years later we saw the poems again (with "the marble center" of the last stanza essentialized as "the old centers") when they were included in *Person, Place and Thing*, by Karl Jay Shapiro, a book that as I recall was the poetic sensation of that year. With the four poems seen in the magazine were several others that my memory treasures as among the best American poems of the century.

Somehow, perhaps because I too was publishing in *POETRY* in those years, we soon came to exchange a few letters; his, from the South Pacific, the photographic army V-letters that gave a title to his next book in 1944.

It was a year later that I gave a talk on his work at St. Michael's College of the University of Toronto, where I was to teach during the following school year. We had a good audience; among them I remember Margaret Avison, who was later to win the Governor General's Medal for her own poetry, and a young instructor by the name of Norrie Frye, who talked to me, after the lecture, about some critical work he had in mind.

Tucked away in my own copy of *Person, Place and Thing* are the scribbled notes of that lecture. As I look back, across forty and more years, on what I said that evening, much of it seems unnecessary now, made obsolete by the subsequent development of poetry, on which Shapiro's own work was to exert so powerful an influence.

I began by reminding the audience how brilliant Shapiro's debut had been, and with what spectacular acclaim he had been received. Louise Bogan had ventured to predict that "his work will become a sort of touchstone for his generation." Allen Tate had written that Shapiro's poetry had "for the first time since T.S. Eliot's arrival more than twenty-five years ago, that final honesty which is rare, unpleasant, and indispensable in a poet of our time." And wasn't it in that same review that Tate had gone so far as to acclaim Shapiro as the hope of American poetry?

I made the observation, less otiose then than now, that he had chosen to avoid those traditional subjects of poetry that would have assured him a friendly readership, preferring instead to affront the taste of this time with titles like "The Snob," "The Glutton," "Mongolian Idiot," "Drug Store," "Honkytonk," "Jew," and "The Fly." Such an angle of vision, the poet says in *The Younger Son*, was "what breaking convention was all about, and why poets and artists were thought cantankerous and ornery." The subjects he chose, I suggested, made the poet's task all the more difficult.

In their handling, some of the poems had been likened to Rilke's *Dinggedichte* or "thing-poems;" Shapiro has admitted that there are parallels. But the great difference between the two is that Rilke's thing-poems, powerful as they are, took fewer chances, coming as they did from those realms of gold long familiar to the Muse: "Die Kathedrale," "Die Gazelle," "Das Einhorn," "Römische Fontäne," "Römische Sarkophage," "San Marco," "Archaïscher Torso Apollos." Shapiro was making not only a daring assault on the convention of poetry, but a strategic one as well: He saw that his subjects had more symbolic relevance for the age in which he lived than those time-hallowed "poetic" ones would have had. As he says in *The Younger Son*, it was not the thing in itself he was interested in, but "the world of the thing."

I mentioned in my early talk that there are dangers in this approach: the poet, like Houdini, may entangle himself in difficulties to show his own dexterity in escaping from them. But in the best poems of this kind, as in so many of Shapiro's, we have a sort of triumph impossible to a more cautious technique: effects of freshness, of power, of a reshuffling of values that leads to a new and truer vision. A poet who deals with refractory materials is preeminently a creator, almost *ex nihilo*, I said, and in his creation leads all of us into a world whose reality we had not suspected.

After such generalities, I went on to exemplify what I took to be the achievement of his poetry by reading and commenting on half a dozen or so works, poems which I thought represented the range of his genius and which seemed to me among the most memorable of those he had done.

The first was "October 1," which begins:

> That season when the leaf deserts the bole
> And half-dead see-saws through the October air
> Falling face-downward on the walks to print

> The decalcomania of its little soul—
> Hardly has the milkman's sleepy horse
> On wooden shoes echoed across the blocks,
> When with its back jaws open like a dredge
> The van comes lumbering up the curb to someone's door
>   and knocks.

That was a stanza that, like much of the poem, memorized itself for me. I liked everything about it: the dramatic anacoluthon of the sentence structure, the risky but convincing animism of the imagery, the plainness, and yet the dignity, of the diction, the use of few but surprising adjectives, the appropriateness of the final fourteener, and the expressiveness of the metrical byplay in the variation on iambic in the first four lines: the spondees, the trochees, the tribrachs, the anapests, and their Mozartean music! The graphic description continues in the second stanza, with its affectionate portrayal of the movers:

> And four black genii muscular and shy
> Holding their shy caps enter the first room
> Where someone hurriedly surrenders up
> The thickset chair, the mirror half awry,
> Then to their burdens stoop without a sound.
> One with his bare hands rends apart the bed,
> One stuffs the china-barrel with stale print,
> Two bear the sofa toward the door with dark funereal tread.

A mode of description preferred by many of the poets we see in today's many poetry journals might read like this:

> Four husky Afro-americans, not saying much,
> come in,
> One of them grabs a chair almost from under
> whoever's sitting in it,
> then a mirror that's hung crooked,
> they do the heavy work in silence,
> one takes the bed apart,
> another stuffs old newspapers in a barrel

> so she can pack dishes in it,
> two others haul the sofa out the door.

But Shapiro is not just snapping a quick Polaroid. What he is doing is what Wordsworth declared his own purpose to be: to take objects from everyday life and throw over them a certain coloring of the imagination. In doing that he transforms the experience through words that are rich and strange in themselves, so that the poem makes a kind of haunting music. What he has done is to take the daily reality that passes and turn it into the art that endures.

"October 1" is not only about moving day; it is not only a description of a single event, but a meditation on "the world of" that event. After two stanzas that cover two more hours of the movers' activity, there finally appears the figure of "the husband in his hat who stands and rests." It seems he is the vague, hurried "someone" of the second stanza, almost a nobody now that he is dispossessed, displaced. There is no one with him.

> He turns with miserable expectant face
> And for the last time enters. On the wall
> A picture-stain spreads from the nail-hole down.
> Each object live and dead has left its trace.
> He leaves his key; but as he quickly goes
> This question comes behind: Did someone die?
> Is someone rich or poor, better or worse?
> What shall uproot a house and bring this care into his eye?

"Scheiden ist der Tod"—the phrase of Goethe's, that might well have been Rilke's, could have served as epigraph for this poem of disorder, expulsion, dispersal. Or even—is it going too far to say?—of the outset of diaspora. It may have been my admiration for the poem that lured me into hyperbole when I said that its theme could almost be aggrandized into Tennyson's "the doubtful doom of humankind."

A poem more explicitly painful is "Hospital," which begins:

> Inside or out, the key is pain. It holds
> The florist to your pink medicinal rose,
> The nickname to the corpse. One wipes it from
> Blue German blades or drops it down the drain;

> The novelist with a red tube up his nose
> Gingerly pets it. Nurse can turn it off.

Perhaps the style could be called "mannered." But if so, it is mannered in a way we recognize as *his* manner. Only strong poets have a manner recognizable as theirs. Who is more mannered than Góngora? Or Milton? Or Hopkins? So individual an impress has been disapproved of by some. A couple of decades after this poem was published, a well known poet of the time could characterize the style of the stanza as "terribly dated" and go on to say "With our recent experience of camp, how easily we could make fun of this. It is an absurd style." Today, though two more decades have gone by, that critical opinion seems more dated than the style of the stanza does. (Just this afternoon I was reading a review in which an editor of *The Economist* declared that "nothing dates faster than allegations of outdatedness.") To me the style of the stanza in question seems justified, if not indeed demanded, by its subject. The stanza that follows, with a simplicity that combines the allusive with the colloquial, may be even better:

> This is the Oxford of all sicknesses.
> Kings have lain here and fabulous small Jews
> And actresses whose legs were always news.
> In this black room the painter lost his sight,
> The crippled dancer here put down her shoes,
> And the scholar's memory broke, like an old clock.

The lines of "Hospital" do, at times, run a high fever: pain is their subject. Shapiro, like Keats, had studied medicine; he knew hospitals, and especially the battlefield hospitals of his South Pacific years with the army.

The poem I turned to next, "The Leg," may have begun in such a hospital. It takes us into the agonized mind of the amputee as he questions and struggles to come to terms with the reality of his pain and his loss, achieving finally what traditional language—though the poet never uses such thumbed and church-worn phrasing—might call a sense of redemption through faith and love.

Among the iodoform, in twilight-sleep,
What have I lost? he first inquires,
Peers in the middle distance where a pain,
Ghost of a nurse, hazily moves, and day,
Her blinding presence pressing in his eyes
And now his ears. They are handling him
With rubber hands. He wants to get up.

One day beside some flowers near his nose
He will be thinking, *When will I look at it?*
And pain, still in the middle distance, will reply,
At what? and he will know it's gone,
O where! and begin to tremble and cry.
He will begin to cry as a child cries
Whose puppy is mangled under a screaming wheel.

Later, as if deliberately, his fingers,
Begin to explore the stump. He learns a shape
That is comfortable and tucked in like a sock.
This has a sense of humor, this can despise
The finest surgical limb, the dignity of limping,
The nonsense of wheel-chairs. Now he smiles to the wall:
The amputation becomes an acquisition.

For the leg is wondering where he is (all is not lost)
And surely he has a duty to the leg;
He is its injury, the leg is his orphan,
He must cultivate the mind of the leg,
Pray for the part that is missing, pray for peace
In the image of man, pray, pray for its safety,
And after a little it will die quietly.

The body, what is it, Father, but a sign
To love the force that grows us, to give back
What in Thy palm is senselessness and mud?
Knead, knead the substance of our understanding
Which must be beautiful in flesh to walk,

> That if Thou take me angrily in hand
> And hurl me to the shark, I shall not die!

In the mind of the patient, we move from numbness and bewilderment to anguished realization, then through a kind of grisly humor to philosophic wonderment about body and soul, and on finally to the ringing confidence of the conclusion, with its recollections of biblical solemnity and exaltation.

There is a kind of strangeness, even of eeriness, in the patient's feeling that he "must cultivate the mind of the leg." A similar strangeness, remote from the confining factuality of many thing-poems, is also felt in "The Twins," which deals with the mysterious complexity of wonder, humor, pathos, and pity in the magnetism of twinship.

> Likeness has made them animal and shy.
> See how they turn their full gaze left and right,
> Seeking the other, yet not moving close;
> Nothing in their relationship is gross,
> But soft, conspicuous, like giraffes. And why
> Do they not speak except by sudden sight?
>
> Sisters kiss freely and unsubtle friends
> Wrestle like lovers; brothers loudly laugh:
> These in a dreamier bondage dare not touch....

There paradoxical nature permits the coupling, in the last two lines, of *Genesis* with *The Comedy of Errors*.

> Theirs is the pride of shouldering each the same
> The old indignity of Esau's race
> And Dromio's denouement of tragic mirth.

Even stranger, more unearthly though of the earth, is the voice that comes to us in "A Cut Flower." The flower itself speaks out of its flower-consciousness, an awareness not quite like our own but which *could* be our own if we had the life-and-death experience of a flower. I do not know of another's poem which so feelingly admits our imagination into the psyche of suffering nature, and in doing so teaches us to endure in a new way the realization of our own mortality.

I stand on slenderness all fresh and fair,
I feel root-firmness in the earth far down,
I catch in the wind and loose my scent for bees
That sack my throat for kisses and suck love.
What is the wind that brings thy body over?
Wind, I am beautiful and sick. I long
For rain that strikes and bites like cold and hurts.
Be angry, rain, for dew is kind to me
When I am cool from sleep and take my bath

Who softens the sweet earth about my feet,
Touches my face so often and brings water?
Where does she go, taller than any sunflower
Over the grass like birds? Has she a root?
These are great animals that kneel to us,
Sent by the sun perhaps to help us grow.
I have seen death. The colors went away,
The petals grasped at nothing and curled tight.
Then the whole head fell off and left the sky.

She tended me and held me by my stalk.
Yesterday I was well, and then the gleam,
The thing sharper than frost cut me in half.
I fainted and was lifted high. I feel
Waist-deep in rain. My face is dry and drawn.
My beauty leaks into the glass like rain.
When first I opened to the sun I thought
My colors would be parched. Where are my bees?
Must I die now? Is this a part of life?

In "The Cloud" Shelley has a cloud speaking at some length, but there is nothing cloudlike in its diction; we could be listening to a meteorologist who had taken a course in metrics. In "Das Veilchen," "Gefunden" and elsewhere Goethe has a flower speak up, but they do so in standard speech, as if they were little Germans. The speech of Shapiro's flower, though akin to human speech, is convincingly eldritch; it comes to us with a floral accent. A poem it might remind us of is the seventh sonnet in the second part of *Die Sonette an Orpheus*, the one beginning Blumen, ihr schliesslich den ordnenden Händen verwandte ... in which the cut flowers recover briefly as the girl's hands ease them into the refreshing vase of water. Though the flowers do not speak, we are permitted to share the feeling of their languishment.

These are the poems I read to my Canadian audience, and more or less what it occurred to me to say about them. Now, so many years later, my admiration and liking for the poems has not lessened in any way. These poems *belong*! They should be in any sensitive reader's personal anthology of the best poems of our time.

~ KS ~

Hans Ostrom

"THIS ISN'T A POEM YET": KARL SHAPIRO THE TEACHER

In 1973 I decided to transfer from a community college to the University of California, Davis—for two reasons. First, I wanted to attend a U.C. campus that my brothers had not attended. (One had gone to Berkeley, the other to Santa Barbara.) Second, I wanted to study with Karl Shapiro. In a critical-reading-of-poetry course that opened the doors of reading to me, I had been astonished by his poems and those of Randall Jarrell—poems like "Auto Wreck" and "Death of the Ball Turrett Gunner." I remember thinking to myself, "So *this* is poetry." And come to find out, one of these Famous Poets actually lived in the Central Valley. We were connected by Interstate 80; I had to go to Davis.

And so I went, infatuated with modern poetry and encased in the painful shyness of a kid from the backwoods of California's Sierra Nevada. Disillusionment lay in wait for me like a spider.

My first disappointment came when I found out that I couldn't enroll in Shapiro's poetry class. The computer booted me out because enrollment was limited to 15 and because a manuscript had to be presented Shapiro during the previous term. I was crest-fallen— but only briefly. After all, the Summer of Love had lasted well into the Seventies. There were plenty of other things to do.

My second disappointment came after I managed to get into his class in the next term, the Winter Quarter of my Discontent. Professor Shapiro wasn't terribly friendly, did not recognize my genius, and when I had passed around my first poem to the workshop (it was about killing rattlesnakes), he pronounced, "This isn't a poem yet."

I was devastated. Then furious. Then determined to please him.

I went on to take three more of Shapiro's courses, repeating the poetry workshop twice, and then taking a Modern Poetics class as a graduate student. Through it all, *this isn't a poem yet* emblemized his teaching. He was both aloof and direct. He could be abrupt, and he could be maddening. But he was a very good teacher. Good because he made you fall out of love with a first draft and ask yourself what you were really trying to do with the poem.

I think Shapiro was aloof for two reasons: first, because he is essentially shy, and second, because the whole poetry workshop *thing* seemed to mystify and sometimes even terrify him. Later he could write an essay (based on a lecture he gave at Davis), "Creative Glut," which summarized his feelings toward the American institution of Creative Writing. He didn't know why so *many* young, tan, laid-back Californians wanted to write poetry; moreover, he didn't think *they* knew why they wanted to write poetry. He seemed *bothered* by all this pullulation.

And so he would simply sit in front of the room and watch us distribute copies of our poems and listen to us talk about them. Often the look on his face was one of a man who had stepped into the wrong room and who was too embarrassed to admit his mistake. At other times he would light and re-light his pipe dozens of times, unable to keep it going. (He was trying to give up cigarettes, and keeping the pipe lit was a skill he could not master.) Occasionally, the class would get into a rip-roaring argument, the personalities of young, tender geniuses flaring into a skirmish. And he would stare wide-eyed at us, as if he were intruding on a family argument of which he wanted no part.

Shapiro did not think of the workshop as his personal platform, so he rarely shared his work with us. Once, though, he shared a draft of "Humanities Building" with us; it was a poem about the sterile concrete monolith that housed the English Department. He had sent it to the *New Yorker*, and the editor wanted a few changes. We geniuses were outraged. How dare he ask Karl Shapiro, our famous teacher, to make changes. Shapiro smiled wryly at us, knowing that we had everything to learn about writing, editing, and publishing. He also told us that he wanted our opinion of the poem because we were one of the best workshops he had ever had. We were surprised by this comment for he had given no other indication that he liked us.

The "rap" among us was that Shapiro didn't do or say enough in the classroom, but mostly what that meant was that we all wanted more praise. Unlike most of my classmates, I had discovered that Karl was at his best as a teacher when a student went to his office with a very specific question. He loathed small-talk, but he liked precise questions. He would spring to life and give a precise—and very helpful—answer. When he found out that I liked Jarrell's poetry, his face lit up, and we talked about Jarrell's penchant for monologues and for helpless victims. And then he told me that when he was editor of *Poetry*, no other poet submitted such immaculate manuscripts as Jarrell's.

Karl seemed both at home and out of place in California. It seemed to me that part of him liked how strange and relaxed life in the Central Valley could be, and it didn't surprise me when he later compared California to Italy in a poem. Davis in particular seemed to suit him because it was an odd mix of a slow farming town like Dixon and a multi-layered city like Berkeley. He seemed to take pride in driving a Chevrolet Corvair after Ralph Nader and Company had managed to stop the production of new ones. In general, the unpretentiousness of Davis seemed to fit him.

On the other hand, he often seemed like an urban visitor to the frontier. In the land of surfing, camping, hiking, mountain-climbing, and river-rafting, here was a bookish, somewhat fastidious poet. He didn't seem terribly interested in California as a *physical* place, a geography. If he wrote about nature, he usually got only as far as his back yard. (That rattlesnake poem of mine, I remember, had the word "manzanita" in it, and he wanted to know what it meant, not knowing that it referred to a kind of brush that covered most of the state; Gary Snyder he isn't.). He approached nature the way he approached most subjects: with a kind of mischievous irony. In a poem in *The New Yorker* dedicated to William Everson, the great Jeffers disciple, it is about, of all things, man-made fireplace logs.

At some point I stopped trying to please Karl and so, of course, pleased him. In the poetics class I wrote a long piece on Jarrell's poetry, and he admired the essay very much. He also seemed genuinely pleased that a poem of mine won a prize in a contest judged by Stephen Spender at the University of Houston. (However, he asked, "What's *he* doing in Texas?") He had a way of monitoring the progress of the few of us who kept writing. Most of all, I sensed that he liked people who continued to read and write—that for him, the work was really the essential thing.

Since then we've exchanged letters several times. I was hired by the University of Puget Sound and discovered that Wilmot Ragsdale, a retired newspaper correspondent who teaches journalism here, knew Karl in Baltimore. When I wrote to tell Karl that "Rags" was here, they revived a correspondence that had ceased decades ago.

In 1983, when Karl was about to retire from full-time teaching, he wrote to tell me that his last poetics seminar would be on Auden. "I've chosen Auden as the meat," he wrote. "It's gonna be fun and work. Auden is endlessly fascinating and slippery."

"Endlessly fascinating and slippery" might also describe Karl Shapiro. He is an academic poet who isn't really academic; an Easterner with a curious *empathy* with the West; a critic who took potshots left (the Beats) and right (Pound and Eliot); a writer who refused to join any "school" (particularly one that would want him); a person who has always thrived on the anomalies of being a "white-haired lover," a "bourgeois poet," and a well-read poet unconcerned about showing off what he has read. I remember him as a teacher who didn't seem to be teaching, but who, by saying things like "This isn't a poem yet," gave me and hundreds of other young writers precisely the sort of clear advice we most needed to hear.

In any case, Karl Shapiro the teacher is among the reasons I have never regretted attending the least ostentatious campus of the University of California. There is something unpredictable and authentic about the Davis campus—and about Karl Shapiro.

~*KS*~

Louis D. Rubin

POET IN ECLIPSE
For Karl Shapiro

1.

Prestigious editors no longer chatter
About him at cocktail parties.
Critics do not debate his latest heresies.
The turncoat anthologists have dropped him
From the canon of those who matter.
There is apathy when his books come out.
It has been years since anyone asked him
Why modern poetry is so difficult.
His own clear translation of the everyday
Has long since given way
To more convolute and crepuscular
Enactments of post-modernist despair.
Elaborate candelabra now flare
Where he was once the Muse's own day-star.

2.

To grow old is our common sacrilege,
For youth prefers its spokesmen cynical,
And he who found himself at center stage
When young, and set himself ablaze in verse,
Must find it spectral to have written well,
And think the worse of fame
For choosing him early on in the game,
Before he knew to be stylishly perverse,
Then let him dangle for a lengthy spell,
Composing what comes to hand
To a diminished public demand.

3.

Still, there are those who see the lucence
Of what he wrote in much we now possess:
He found the language that could bring alive
The everyday dignity of our town,
Learned to make the astounding adjective
Infuse the colorless neutral noun
And called into luminous elegance
What all had thought drab hitherto.
He claimed our untitled circumstance
For poetry, fixed its impress
Equally for high romance
As any ivied castle, campus, salon,
Requiring no prelate nor Helicon
Nor claim to privileged view.
Did not sneer at those
Who thought a civilization worth saving,
And scoffed at the clever self-serving,
The smugly righteous pose
Of the fashionable hierophants:
Our bourgeois poet-heretic-Jew.

4.

Who shun all facile metonymy
May practice a singular astronomy.
Observe the tilting planets sway
In fixed galactic orbit around the sun
See what is masked from sight
Turn bright again by night,
Decline all rumor of oblivion.
So language holds its luster
And words in luminous cluster
Create their own perihelion,
Remain visible, will not fade away.
No matter that most telescopes
Focus upon an evening's ornate flare,

Louis D. Rubin

A pyrotechnic screed of garish tropes,
What's lucid and radiant
Survives past all accident
When darkness clarifies the air.

~*KS*~

Robert Phillips

A NATIONAL MONUMENT

On December 13, 1990, at the New York Historical Society in New York City, The Academy of American Poets presented Karl Shapiro in its annual "Education of the Poet" series. The following remarks were made by Robert Phillips as an introduction of Mr. Shapiro:

Recently I found myself watching a TV quiz show. The trivia question was, "what is our only moveable national monument" As the clock ticked away, an answer sprang to my mind : **KARL SHAPIRO**.

According to the game show host, the correct answer was, The San Francisco Cable Cars. But consider *my* answer for a moment. Certainly Karl Shapiro is moveable; so mush so, he and his wife, the translator Sophie Wilkins, move their household from Manhattan to California and back again once or twice every year. And certainly he *is* one of our national monuments. But one more like Mt. Rushmore than the cute little cable cars. For like Rushmore, Shapiro has loomed large on our horizon for decades, since publication of his first trade poetry book, *Person, Place and Thing* in 1942. Like Rushmore, his work is solid, chiseled, artful and permanent. Those qualities earned him both the Pulitzer Prize and the Bollingen Prize. And curiously like Mt. Rushmore, he even has several faces.

The first face is that of the lyric poet, a poet in the tradition of Auden. Few have written better formal poems in our time. But his are formal poems with a difference—the difference being audacious subject matter. I remember the shock with which I encountered my first Shapiro poem. It was in the big maroon Louis Untermeyer anthology, *Modern American Poetry*, one of the vademecums of my generation. I was an undergraduate, the anthology was the text, and I cracked it open to a poem titled "University." There I read,

> "to hurt the Negro and avoid the Jew
> Is the curriculum ...

Hurt the Negro? Avoid the Jew? In the first lines of a lyric poem? This was brave stuff, particularly in the 1940s. Next I read a poem titled "Buick," which was sexy and razzy and ultimately, I suspected, not about an automobile at all. Other poems, once read, were never forgotten for their mixture of hard reality and soft musicality. You know the poems I mean—"Auto Wreck," "Hospital," "Haircut," Cadillac," "Adam & Eve," "The Fly," "Mongolian Idiot" the list goes on and on.

The second face on this monument is very different from the first. I'll never forget the dismay with which I initially read Shapiro's seventh collection, *The Bourgeois Poet* (1964). Expecting more of what had come before, I found instead the poet was experimenting with—of all things!—prose poems, the two traditional attributes of poetry, rhyme and versification, had been totally abandoned. Oh, the poems had a form all right: Each was shaped like the State of Oklahoma, with a panhandle sticking out on the left! It took me years to appreciate Shapiro's achievement in that book. Some critics have never caught up to it yet. but his refusal to keep repeating himself should be applauded. "Find out what you can do well," Jean Cocteau said, "Then do something else." Shapiro did. His prose poems are models for the genre. At the time of publication he was accused of imitating Allen Ginsberg. What critics didn't realize was, Shapiro was abstracting his own formal background. Ginsberg had no formal background to abstract.

Shapiro's third face is that of the critic—and what an original and independent critic he is. Even the titles of his collections of essays are upbraiding: *In Defense of Ignorance*, *To Abolish Children*, *The Poetry Wreck*....His essays are so bold, so unyielding, when I first met the man I expected to be terrified. Instead I met a gentleman in both senses of that word. I couldn't believe this was the essayist who had called Henry MIller "Gandhi with a penis," or the one who had said of T.S. Eliot that he was a successful critic but a failed poet, a theologian gone astray. There are entire English Departments who have not forgiven him for that.

The fourth face is the autobiographer. In recent years, Mr. Shapiro has published his two-volume autobiography with the over-all title *Poet*, and the individual volumes subtitled *The Younger Son* (1988) and *Reports of my Death* (1990). Written in the unorthodox third person, the autobiography is funny, candid, outrageous and original.

We can add one more face to this monument, giving Shapiro one more than even Rushmore. That is the face of the editor. He edited both *Poetry* magazine and *Prairie Schooner* for many years. His editorial standards were high and international in scope. In addition, he has edited several influential textbooks on poetry and prosody, among them *A Prosody Handbook* (1965) and *Prose Keys to Modern Poetry* (1962).

But enough is enough. Obviously we are dealing with a very complex individual. I'm pleased to present my friend and a true apostle of poetry, the monumental Karl Shapiro.

~KS~

David R. Slavitt

AN HOMAGE AND A POEM TO KARL

English professors, who aren't stupid, have raised an interesting set of questions about influence. If there is such a thing as a tradition how does one poet influence another, how does an older poet's work condition or enable or restrict or affect the work of a younger poet? But the professors lead lives that are misleadingly orderly, too compartmentalized and too linear. Often, then, they miss the answers they have been seeking or, worse, twist them beyond recognizability or utility.

In a tribute such as this to Karl Shapiro, I am happy to offer a poem, which is not about Karl Shapiro but was enabled by him. I can see his name in the watermark of the paper. I can hear the timbre of his voice in the voice that spoke to me—not the words of the poem but those of the suggestion that the poem was do-able.

It may not be a good poem. I haven't yet decided that, haven't lived with it long enough. But it is a nervy poem, brash or at least impish, in the way that Karl Shapiro has taught us it is sometimes good to be. The risks here are certainly smaller than those at the other end of the spectrum, in that pompous Eliotic poetry that, in Karl's words (in "The Career of the Poem") "is supposed to be sacred, hieratic poetry, and this I consider evil. We should strip the poet of his false honors, false titles and false powers."

This is a curious and subversive thing for a poet to be saying, but then, on second thought, not so. It is the poet trying to snatch back from the wardens of culture the privileges that have been stolen from him—the privilege of deciding what a poem is and what it can do and how it ought to do that. Karl is against "the rule of Culture over art," and says that "The new poet is always the one who outwits the guardians of the prevalent systems—and mostly because he is not even aware of their existence."

So, to begin with, there is that cantankerous, almost rebellious spirit, what Hemingway called the "built-in, portable, fool-proof shit detector," which is the writer's most valuable asset. Then there is the anti-poetic rhythm of some of Karl's prose poems from *The Bourgeois Poet* with their deceptive plainsong quality. But there are accidentals, too. Karl's wife, Sophie Wilkins, has translated several of Thomas Bernhard's novels, and on the strength of this, because of my regard for her—whom I met, of course, through Karl, so I owe him for her too—I read *Corrections*, which has a peculiar incantational battiness that must have been a challenge to even so adept a translator as she. (I say this because I cannot imagine a German original any better or more natural, or more hypnotic and beguiling as it raves on about "Altensam, and everything connected with Altensam, and Hoeller's garret, and the cone in the middle of the Kobernausser forest.")

The result? Or, more precisely and less clearly, the after effect? A kind of verbal giddiness, I should say, that lasted for some days. An exhilaration and a sense of the sad power that raving can sometimes manifest. And then a coincidence—in the shape of an irresistible offer from the History Book Club: buy these four books at amazing bargain prices with no obligation to make further purchases ever—dropped a copy of Jonathan Spence's *The Search for Modern China* into my lap. I had liked the title and delighted to imagine the appropriate text: "Find Japan. Then look for the first country to the left of it, that big blobby one before you get to Russia!" (Besides, my daughter had studied with Spence at Yale and had liked his course, and because of that I'd read *The Death of Woman Wang* and *The Memory Palace of Matteo Ricci*.)

So there I am, reading away at Spence's bleak chronicle of the collapse of the Ming dynasty, and with Bernhard resonating in my head, and I am on the way back from the post office and feeling the rhythm of walking. (Robert Penn Warren used to compose while swimming, getting the rhythm of the line right and then scribbling it out into a notebook at the end of the pool.) I find myself saying, over and over again, "suffering, suffering, suffering, more suffering, really terrible suffering, a slight improvement, flood, more suffering, suffering, suffering ..."

Something like that. Nearly babble—which is where Richard Wilbur says we must go to find the source of our poems, the baby talk from which we have never quite emerged. So baby-babble in which I know the meanings of the words but don't let them oppress me too much. "Suffering, suffering, suffering ..."

I think of my joke title of How to Find ... No, "The Search for Modern China." and I think of a title for my babble: "A Short History of Modern China." (Or "A Shorter History ..."? But a shorter history is less short than a short history, as a younger poet is older than a young poet, and I have done that joke already in the title of *Eight Longer Poems*.)

The poem, almost inadvertently, is already there. All that remains at this point is to have the nerve to insist that it may be worth putting onto paper, may be worth calling a poem. May have some reality, never mind value!

And there, again, Karl has been invaluable in another, quite different but important way. There are some poets whom early honors have killed, making them take themselves too seriously. Eliot's praise for Delmore Schwartz hurt him more than it helped. I have been spared that kind of praise and attention. But there are a few people for whose regard I have regard, and who have enabled me to think of myself, if I have to face the question, as a writer of some worth. "If I say it's a poem, it's a poem!" is a nervy assertion to make but nerve is a part of this business. So I switch the machine on and click on "New" which is always a brash gesture. And the poem follows. I offer it to Karl, not because I am convinced that it is so wonderful but because I am not, and because it is his friendship that has enabled me even to dare it.

"The Anxiety of Influence" is, I think, Harold Bloom's title—which sounds rather like a tract for AA, actually. But there is also such a thing as the Intimacy of Influence, the Gratitude of Influence, the Affluence of Influence, and even, Lord help us, the Joy of Influence. In Joy, then:

AN EXTREMELY SHORT HISTORY OF CHINA

T'ang Dynasty

Suffering, suffering, squalor, suffering, flood, suffering, suffering, really severe suffering, war, suffering, suffering, drought, famine, suffering, brutal suffering, really terrible suffering, a slight diminution of suffering, a few years of reasonable life, the birth of some hope, the revival of the arts and crafts, and then corruption, disaster, war, and flood, drought and more suffering.

David R. Slavitt

Five Dynasties era

Suffering, suffering, squalor, suffering, flood, suffering, suffering, really severe suffering, war, suffering, suffering, drought, famine, suffering, brutal suffering, really terrible suffering, a slight diminution of suffering, a few years of reasonable life, the birth of some hope, the revival of the arts and crafts, and then corruption, disaster, war, and flood, drought and more suffering.

Sung Dynasty

Suffering, suffering, squalor, suffering, flood, suffering, suffering, really severe suffering, war, suffering, suffering, drought, famine, suffering, brutal suffering, really terrible suffering, a slight diminution of suffering, a few years of reasonable life, the birth of some hope, the revival of the arts and crafts, and then corruption, disaster, war, and flood, drought and more suffering.

Yüan Dynasty

Suffering, suffering, squalor, suffering, flood, suffering, suffering, really severe suffering, war, suffering, suffering, drought, famine, suffering, brutal suffering, really terrible suffering, a slight diminution of suffering, a few years of reasonable life, the birth of some hope, the revival of the arts and crafts, and then corruption, disaster, war, and flood, drought and more suffering.

Ming Dynasty

Suffering, suffering, squalor, suffering, flood, suffering, suffering, really severe suffering, war, suffering, suffering, drought, famine, suffering, brutal suffering, really terrible suffering, a slight diminution of suffering, a few years of reasonable life, the birth of some hope, the revival of the arts and crafts, and then corruption, disaster, war, and flood, drought and more suffering.

Ch'ing Dynasty

Suffering, suffering, squalor, suffering, flood, suffering, suffering really severe suffering, war, suffering, suffering, drought, famine, suffering, brutal suffering, really terrible suffering, a slight diminution of suffering, a few years of reasonable life, the birth of some hope, the revival of the arts and crafts, and then corruption, disaster, war, and flood, drought and more suffering..

Republic Of China

Suffering, suffering, squalor, suffering, flood, suffering, suffering, really severe suffering, war, suffering, suffering, drought, famine, suffering, brutal suffering, really terrible suffering, a slight diminution of suffering, a few years of reasonable life, the birth of some hope, the revival of the arts and crafts, and then corruption, disaster, war, and flood, drought and more suffering.

People's Republic of China

Suffering, suffering, squalor, suffering, flood, suffering, suffering, really severe suffering, war, suffering, suffering, drought, famine, suffering, brutal suffering, really terrible suffering, a slight diminution of suffering, a few years of reasonable life, the birth of some hope, the revival of the arts and crafts, and then corruption, disaster, war, and flood, drought and more suffering.

~ KS ~

John Wheatcroft

Love And War

To Karl, Comrade in Arms

Blood on our hands, blood of our buddies
innocent blood, blood of the beaten.
Still in our eye, fire flash
from hits on water and land, in sky.
Concussive the blast of our own big guns,
then rushing into our ear
shrieks and moans and whimpers heard
only in our nightmares. We smelled
the stink of flesh we'd never seen
but knew we'd roasted in their oven cities.

Homeward bound, tied up in Hawaii,
we sprinted down the gangway
to open arms and legs—
erect we were as ack-ack guns
scanning the skies for Bettys,
by the time we had undone our thirteen buttons
in the shack of her we picked:
the one with two gold teeth and a rose
tattooed on her thigh; the pear-hipped one
with moss on her belly; the still half-child
who twittered, "Say-lo, say-lo, am I
good for you?" while her little tawny feet
fluttered above my head like butterflies.

So many years it's taken me
to learn those oceanic girls
who like salt water lapped and laved
and solaced us, the wounded ones,
were peris, heavenly beings imprisoned
in liquid flesh. Not to reward us

for forced continence while we
devoutly killed. Nor to take from us
the edge before we bedded with
home bodies we'd defended. Rather,
to put us to love's test: could we
touch them gently? use them kindly?
be grateful for their favor? give
beyond the pittance they saw fit
to ask, those angels who
tendered us their selves?

~ *KS* ~

Peter Viereck

ON KARL SHAPIRO

    Karl Shapiro has turned out to be the finest of his generation of poets. It is often called "the tragic generation" by fetishists of private biography because so many were felled young by madness, suicide, alcohol. Catastrophe—chic ought to be irrelevant, pro or con, in judging their oeuvre objectively. The time for such objective distancing has now come. All had their merits—Lowell, Jarrell, Berryman, Schwartz—but Shapiro's poems survive best of all. The test of time—a rereading of each one—makes that clear; he is the one who'll be longest remembered. Re time: lose no time reading critics of theories and schools when you can use the time better to reread the work itself, the work of that major creator, Karl Shapiro. Read, read, read.

~ KS ~

Ken Stone

PHENOMENON

To Karl Shapiro

The sure words brilliantly confirmed
Nature herself remembers *the phenomenon.*
Every reader a witness to greatness
Made clear phrase after phrase.

Like visitors to a theatre,
First time experience breathing
The freshness of thought, new-born
And warm to the touch.

We live in the glow of flame
Bright and golden, saturated
Fullness of form and rhyme
Made joyful over time by your love.

~KS~

Ken Stone

WORSHIP

To Karl Shapiro

Now wonderous spectre,
steal my soul with your words
as if it were a prize I could
freely give as your gratuity:
I dare write this humble greeting
in my own hand; remembering
how beautiful freedom really is:
Your writing a *love letter*
reaching beyond mere words
and all your imperfections
and perfections to the scenery
aglow in the magnitude of your grace:
The strength of gracious smiles
and thoughts seem as open doors
into time and other-space:
Because your love is whole....

~ KS ~

John Brugaletta

SACRIFICE

For Karl Shapiro

What snow would fall more pure and cold on the mountains,
What muscular mares would foal, fig trees bear,
If I were to turn my back upon the crowd
And offer up my art to Jaweh's mouth?

And who are they who watch? Here an angel,
Sentenced to the earth for loving fools,
Approves my futile act, recalls his own.
Here another counts the meter's cost.
Another wonders if the metaphors
Will sensitize correctly arrant men.

Yet something eats the doves I bleed and leave.
And in the silence, in the cold, I sense
A voice is speaking, though I cannot hear.
I turn. The crowd is gone, the snow is deep.

~ 𝒦𝒮 ~

Robert Phillips

KARL SHAPIRO AND HIS LATEST POEMS

Literary fame is often an ephemeral thing. Take, for instance, the writers chosen by George P. Elliott for his influential anthology, *15 Modern Poets*. (originally published by Holt, Rinehart & Winston in 1956, my copy is a 1965 sixth printing; doubtless there were later printings as well.) Of the fifteen, is the excellent Winfield Townley Scott read anymore? Or Hyam Plutzik? James Schevill? Even Delmore Schwartz has become a literary oddity, remembered more for details of his tragic life than for his poetry.

Among Elliott's fifteen poets was also Karl Shapiro. Shapiro has received some of the highest honors this country has to offer a poet—the Pulitzer Prize, the Bollingen Prize, Consultantship in Poetry to the Library of Congress, and membership in the American Academy of Arts and Letters. And yet, of the so-called "Mid-Century American Poets" (the title of another influential anthology, this one edited by John Ciardi), Shapiro also seems to have somewhat slipped from view. Certainly there are not the number of books and essays about him which have created entire industries about Robert Lowell, Theodore Roethke, Randall Jarrell, John Berryman, and the younger Sylvia Plath. Of course, Shapiro is very much still with us, whereas Lowell and the others mentioned have met with premature deaths—the latter three by their own hands. Not only is the body of work complete in their cases, but there is a certain glamour attached to their reputations not accorded the living.

Another reason why Shapiro does not seem to be mentioned in the same company as Lowell *et al.* might be his conscious decision to keep a low profile over the past decades. He has been a reputation rather than a presence. While Lowell was marching in Washington or chastising the President, while Berryman was drunkenly flying to every major campus for reading, Shapiro was living in Nebraska and later Davis, California. The East—Manhattan and Boston, with their power politics—has never been a part of his life. He may have paid for this in ebbing influence and readership.

Most recently, even the choice of publisher may have cost Shapiro recognition. In 1984 he published his first collection in six years. It was brought out not by Random House, Shapiro's publisher for decades. Instead, he gave it to a small publisher in the South. When the book appeared, it did not bear the address of the publisher (should one wish to order a copy). It did not even bear a price. Nor did the jacket copy inform the reader—assuming the book *found* a reader—that the volume entitled *Love & War Art & God,* was in the main an updated version of Shapiro's selected poems. Subtitled "The Poems of Karl Shapiro," it actually did contain new and previously uncollected poems, some not even published in magazines. Yet, the book received scant critical notice. It seems unthinkable that a new Lowell or Bishop title would be given such cavalier attention, by publisher and by critics.[1]

Love & War Art & God is the fourth volume in which Shapiro has selected and reprinted old material together with new. (I exclude *Poems of a Jew* [1958], in which he gathered all his poems on Jewish themes, extracted mostly from volumes that had nothing to do with the topic.) His first attempt at a book of selected poems was *Poems 1940-1953* [1953], which contained 116 poems taken from three previous collections, plus 18 more recent poems. *Selected Poems* [1968] held 179 previous poems and 24 new and uncollected ones. A decade later came *Collected Poems, 1940-1978*, which for a less prolific poet would have been the definitive edition, with 224 earlier poems, 15 new and uncollected ones.

Then comes *Love & War Art & God*, which by my count contains 14 new poems and 72 earlier ones. The book, as its title suggests, is arranged in four sections, each dealing with a separate Shapiro theme or pre-occupation. Within these sections, the poet has arranged the poems alphabetically by title, which gives the book a marvelously cosmopolitan texture: "Bath-Sheba" sits next to "Buick," "The Fly" next to "The Leg," "Homecoming" next to "Hospital." Given the diversity and catholicism of Shapiro's taste, the quixotic arrangement works and makes for fresh and surprising juxtapositions.

It is interesting to speculate on Shapiro's method of selection for this book. The newer poems, obviously, are those written since *Collected Poems, 1940-1978*. But with what guidelines did he choose from over the two-hundred earlier poems? Subject matter (love, war, etc.) had much to do with the decision, in addition to regard for quality. But after a time, personal favoritism must be the guide. With the early work he seems to have resisted the urge to revise in the interests of euphony or sense or both, an attitude I applaud. After all, many of Shapiro's poems are new set-pieces. One would hate to see them tampered with. Time will never forgive what John Crowe Ransom and Marianne Moore did to some of their early poems when they reprinted them late in life. In the case of Auden, he simply banished altogether from the canon some of his best poems.

Under the heading "Love," one finds the strongest poems in this collection: "And Now, the Weather," "Essay on Chess," "Girls Fighting, Broadway," "Homewreck," "Morning," "Premises," "The Back," and "The Spider Mums." Several of these are conventional love poems. "Morning" and "Premises" celebrate a new romantic attachment. "The Back" employs synedoche, with "one of the foremost organs of beauty / Especially in women" standing for all the poet adores in his beloved. He concludes, "On this small platonic continent / Let love graze." Even more moving is the chess poem, in which the game, its preparations, execution, and aftermath, is emblematic of the relationship between lover and beloved:

> What really matters are the sounds I hear
> When you clear the board and put the pieces back in the box,
> And the verdict of your eyes when you look up at me.

This is poetry worthy of Shapiro at his best.

The downside of love is portrayed in "Homewreck," while "Girls Fighting, Broadway," recreates a Manhattan tableau which, to passersby, may appear to be kissing but which in reality is a battle royal. The poem, like Shapiro's early war poem, "Scyros," is built of many images without interrelating statements. He has omitted all punctuation, even a final period, which recreates the street fight in all its breathlessness.

All these later poems are written in a modern idiom. There are even allusions to Reagan and to the Horchow catalogue (the latter being a fancy Texas mail-order concern). They are written in a more relaxed style and technique than the earlier formal poems which made Shapiro famous, such as "Adam and Eve" and "Recapitulations," with their a, b, a, b, rhyme schemes. On the other hand, they are more often more dense than the poems of *The Bourgeois Poet* (1964), that book in which he evolved a poetic-paragraph form eschewing not only rhyme but meter as well. At that time, Shapiro proclaimed both of those traditional attributes of poetry were "nonessential and artificial impediments of the poetic process." Of course, in the loose sonnets of *White-Haired Lover* (1968), his next single collection, he more or less returned from his apostasy from conventional prosody. The poems in *Love & War* show him sometimes using rhyme and meter, sometimes not. In "The Spider Mums," a poem of three five-line stanzas, only the last two lines of each quintet rhyme, and the inversion in the last line of the last stanza creates a comic effect: "Though permanent flowers aren't." Here Shapiro risks a departure into light verse in a way he has seldom attempted.

Under the category of "War," we find just one new poem cohabiting with those early World War II poems such as "Troop Train," "Elegy for a Dead Soldier," and "Full Moon: New Guinea." The new poem harkens back to an even earlier war, that between the States, "Grant's Tomb Revisited" contrasts quotations from the item of Grant's funeral ("One million people turned out for the event. . .") with the tomb's present unkempt and unvisited state. Shapiro manages to make of Grant a latter-day Ozymandians, whose monument is a colossal wreck.[2]

The section Shapiro devotes to "Art "includes the poems "Impact," "Poet in Residence," "The Pigeons, "and "The Sawdust Logs." In the first of these he reveals that the suburban and the sacred can be one, just as in "The Pigeons" he delicately explores the role of chance in the Universe. "The Sawdust Logs" is one of his finest poems, ranking with the best of the love poems in the first section. Here the poet tries, in Frost's term, to know what to make of a diminished thing. The price of wood gone up "and the price of fire soared / Sky-high. . .", the poet buys instead some sawdust logs—a poor ubstitute for the real thing. At first the narrator rationalizes,

> A lover of oak and almond and eucalyptus
> I felt a little ashamed. Another substitute.
> Well, why shouldn't sawdust have its day?

Soon enough he finds out why. The logs emit no gunshots, no fire fountains. "An honest fake electric fire with a shadow fan / Would be better than this."

Symbol of all the compromises and the synthetic in the modern world, the sawdust logs in the morning are their own elegy:

> ...hardly visible, dust mice, cigaret ash,
> With a welfare smell,
> Or perhaps, like crematorium ash,
> Too mortal and too fine,
> All but a trace, joyless, eternal,
> Consumed, consumed, consumed.

The poem is a meditation on the American proverb, "They don't make things like they used to"—even those things which one used to gather "for free."

"The Cathedral Bells" is the sole new poem in the final section which is devoted to poems on God." Like the poems on Grant's Tomb and Broadway girls, it reflects Shapiro's environment during this period. In 1984, he began to spend half the year in Manhattan, living on the upper West Side with his third wife in a book-lined flat over-looking the Cathedral of St. John the Divine. This poem is a direct response to that venue. Within its seven stanzas of varying length, the unfinished cathedral undergoes a sea-change (literally). From being an inspiration to finish unfinished things ("I understand the vocational clamber of bees..."), it becomes a fantasy, a vehicle for escape. With its nave as tall as the *Queen Mary*, the cathedral—indeed, the entire island of Manhattan—becomes a ship. (Shapiro may unconsciously have been echoing Auden's "On This Island." In that poem Auden describes the English cathedrals as "Luxury liners laden with souls, / Holding to the east their hulls of stone.")

Whether viewed as goad or fantasy, the cathedral is a symbol not to be totally trusted by the poet, being a "tired endeavor, not quite in good faith / Since the rich have moved away." The latter refrain, in variation, is twice repeated, like a litany or chant from the cathedral itself. The poem is a collage of the secular and sacred, artistic and quotidian.

Buried within yet another "selected poems," these newer works have failed to command the attention they deserve. Evidencing the spirited wit, wide-ranging intellect, emotional power and certain artistry that are characteristic of Shapiro's lifework, they show us that the poet's powers are undiminished in his seventh decade. It is a work that has earned him a place beside his more glittering legendary contemporaries, Lowell and Berryman, Bishop and Roethke.

NOTES

[1] *Love & War Art & God.* Winston-Salem, NC: Stuart Wright, Berkeley, Ca, 1984.

[2] I can't resist adding that when Anouk Aimee, the French film actress, visited New York, her chauffeur proudly pointed out Grant's Tomb. *Cary* Grant?" she inquired with great concern. As reported in the Talk of the Town" column, *The New Yorker*, LXI, 18 (June 24, 1985). 24-27.

~ 𝒦𝒮 ~
Sophie Wilkins
SERIOUSLY MEETING KARL SHAPIRO

In January 1993 it was fifty-one years since I first met Karl Shapiro.
He came to say goodbye, a month after Pearl Harbor, to Alvin Meyer, his best friend ever since Alvin had gone to medical school in Baltimore where Karl was born—in the hospital where Edgar Allan Poe died—to the rooming-house in Long Island City where Alvin and I shared a tiny room that just held a double bed, a typewriter, an arm-chair, an alcove for the two-ring gasburner, the bare necessities. The typewriter, an ancient Underwood, had seen me through my master's thesis on Franz Kafka, and my first book-length translation, Curt Riess's *Underground Europe*, 1942, for which I had just been paid, so I had recklessly bought a new outfit, a pleated gray skirt and green sweater-blouse, though there was no further income in sight. But it was such a momentous occasion, our first guest, my first real live poet—Alvin had shown me his inscribed copy of Karl's first book, privately printed in 1935, *Poems*, impressively accomplished for a man barely out of his teens then.

We had hardly begun to believe that the country was at war full-time on both sides of the globe, the draft was looming—Alvin was a psychiatric intern at Bellevue and the army was sucking up young doctors like a vacuum cleaner—and here was Karl, in uniform, about to be shipped off to the Pacific wars, lamb to the slaughter. He sat on the bed, back to the wall at the window-end of the room, deep in conversation with his old friend on the typing chair opposite, while I, at the foot-end near the door, stared at his handsome profile with those wraparound eyes and failed to follow what was being said, fascinated but quite out of it. When Alvin decided to run out for drinks, I was left alone with our guest, wildly searching for something to say till I caught sight of an old Franz Hals print of The Bohemian girl, that apple-cheeked bushy haired peasant beauty with the dimply smile (no teeth showing, though; could the tightlipped smiles of those classic beauties have been hiding rotten teeth?) over the ancient dead fireplace, and I said: "A Mona Lisa of the People, isn't she?" The search-light glare of those luminous brown eyes, saying distinctly:

"What's she trying to pull?" remains forever imprinted in the darkroom of my mind. I sensed that my outdated thirties' ideology was showing, in its then current Popular Front version. At long last Alvin returned with a bottle. Glass in hand, Karl spoke of his girl, Evalyn, who would be coming to New York City to continue the publishing of his poems in his absence, and would need friends. Karl's matter-of-fact leave-taking left us abashed, in awe of his mission, his uncertain fate, the sheer distance he was about to put between us and himself; distance in more ways than one, as it turned out.

Soon there was a letter from Evalyn, which must be quoted in its entirety, typography—the e.e. cummings influence—and all, it is so rich in the atmospherics of that time for us:

tues 12pm
feb 17

sophie, it is good to be able to write you, since you have become more than an endeared synonym to all that is ny, or at least my part accompaniment. i have all of karls words here in my lap - of his visits to you and alvin and ny. by the stealth of time and active regulations of the army, and the temporariness of the entire setup, i have not been able to get my feet on the high step that wd take me up there. i have karl's assurance, which is so often accountable eagerness, that you wd and generously share yr room, the room that he described so clearly. i have no plans - only that i want to touch the face of this place - and meet those that are his friends. i wd like to sledge the streets and take hold of a thousand eyes. the ailment that wd help me to remember the city. the cathode to help to keep it bright. i love this city, sophie, like the key that turns the lock free, and the air that shoves through the open window. the free. does this sound young and memorial? i don't know how it sounds, but i know how it feels. i shd like to leave sat. about 10.30 and ill call you when i arrive, *if* theres no demurrer from you. i hope karl will be there, even tho hes written hes headed somewhere unknown tho he believes ny. hell call me before the weekend tho. ive written him that i intend to leave this weekend. and youll probably hear from him in the meantime. hes still somewhat delerious from his scrimmages. and so am i with the possibilities. my love to the minstrelled alvin, and to you honesty, which is my thanks. please write me.

Evalyn

How could Karl have described that closet-sized room, with barely space to pass between the furniture, as a place she could want to stay, indefinitely as it seemed, with another person or two? Anyway, how could I 'demur'? Evalyn came that Saturday, the 24th of February, eve of my dreaded 27th birthday, to Bellevue (easier to find) where she spent the day with Alvin, who brought her home in time for me to take them to dinner. (In those days interns were paid $18.-a month.) She and Karl had met just ten days before he was drafted in 1940, by which time Alvin had begun his general internship in New York, so we were both seeing her for the first time: Evalyn of the gentle southern accents, the Gibson girl prettiness and femininity, so appealingly at a loss in the looming gray city, so bravely taking it on, alone, armed only with a sheaf of poems by a virtual unknown though already published in the New Directions series of Five Young American Poets, taking on the notorious literary and publishing mafias. Love in gossamer besieging an impregnable fortress! Evalyn and Alvin—even their names rhymed!—were soon immersed in each other, they had heard so much about each other from Karl, they had Karl and Baltimore and mutual friends in common. At one point Alvin suddenly asked Evalyn, like the forthright, privileged psychoanalyst he was going to be, "How old are you?" Softly she said, "Twenty-two ..." and with a side-glance at me, "... but I feel much older ..." When I slipped Alvin the money for the check, it transpired that Evalyn had nowhere to stay. Alvin offered to go back to Bellevue on his night off. He was on 48-hour duty, which meant that I saw him once in three days, when he didn't have to go to Brooklyn to see his parents or anything. It could be a week or more before I would see him again, we had not been together long, I was obsessed with him. I was a year older, deeply unsure of him, and the thought of waking up on my birthday with Evalyn in my bed instead of him was insupportable. There was a special problem too: When my father left Vienna, where I was born, for New York, I was six years old, with two much older sisters and my mother, who were always talking with each other over my head, women's talk, which I despised (I had learned to read at the age of four) and I had learned to loathe the big female nudes with their heavy breasts, having to share my bed with one or the other; the prospect of turning into one of those myself was a terror that made suicide an attractive way out.

Yet I found myself, that night, abed between Alvin and Evalyn, side by side across the width of the bed with our heads to the wall and our feet hanging down or sticking out, like some medieval sword between a man and a woman forbidden to love one another. It was the antithesis of an orgy. I never slept for a nanosecond that night. At daylight I finally crawled out from between them, asleep on either side of me, and crouched on a hassock, head between my knees, acutely depressed, crying floods of silent tears from sheer loss of resistance. After what seemed hours, I could hear Evalyn murmuring: "Little Miss Muffet sat on a tuffet ..." and later, the three of us up, she said as if to herself, "Sophie has a wooden face ..." a remark which made a profound difference to the rest of my life, hard as that is to explain, though I must try: I had always chafed at the irregular planes of my slavic (or mongol?) face, having an extremely pretty older sister in whom the same genes, the same family features, had bloomed into an apotheosis; it was a chronic inward chafing for which I had no words. Evalyn's remark gave me the words, gave me a concept: when it occurred to me that I could best be portrayed in a woodcut, I was reconciled to my fate, I could live with it. Helen Keller's childhood discovery of words as an empowerment at that famous moment when she connected the sensation of water on her hands with a code tapped out in that hand comes to mind. Even if Evalyn was mostly inspired by the set, despairing look my features must have worn under those circumstances, she has always been to me what the French would call *une femme formidable*. As indeed she proved to be soon enough, in her handling of Karl's literary affairs in his absence. But at the time, another such night was unthinkable, and we saw Evalyn off on the train to Baltimore that

Sophie Wilkins

Sunday, the 25th of February, 1942.

What followed was much correspondence, with Karl in New Guinea and Australia, with Evalyn in Baltimore and later New York, when we had landed in Minnesota. Alvin's draft notice had arrived one day later than his orders from the Public Health Service to be posted as prison psychiatrist at the Federal Correctional Institution in Sandstone, MN. It was a no-walls, no-clubs minimal custody prison used mainly for conscientious objectors, religious and other, politicals like the fifteen Trotskyites led by Jimmy Cannon, Felix Morrow et al., and the like, where in 1943 J.F. Powers arrived, as a Catholic C.O., a week after I had read his first brilliant story, "Lions, Harts, and Leaping Does" in *Accent*. In those seven-month Minnesota winters there was plenty of time to write letters, many of them V-Letters sent to that APO number in San Francisco, many to Evalyn in New York overseeing the publication of *Person Place & Thing* and *V-Letter*. Before we left New York Evalyn had shown us the original blue one-piece letter on which Karl had handwritten the poem for which years later the book was named, as his actual letter to her of that date. It was a revelation, after the well-crafted but conventional poems of seven years before, to witness the birth of that strong, distinctive, sovereign voice transforming the soft coal of experience into diamonds of poems, by knowing how to take hold of it, how to compress it into polished facets of colorful meaning. "V-Letter" is not a "great poem", or one of KS's best, but the boldness and candor with which it fuses the intimacies of a love-letter with the threatening atmosphere of war by means of such ordinary domestic concerns as "groceries upon a shelf" "metal minutes of your pay" "drab makings of a room" the daring to use "words that creep and sting like insects" and to expose ambivalence, conflict, trouble, in what could turn out to be one's last will and testament—no place to take chances, no place for ambiguities—makes it outstanding, and above all, liberating. When *Person Place & Thing* appeared the same year, I was moved to memorize "Scyros" and I sent Karl a translation into German of "Necropolis."

Sophie Wilkins

Nekropolis*

Ja, noch im Tod florieren sie, im Tode
Wo Lust verstummt und Stolz zunichte wird,
Gedeihen sie und krönen ihren Hügel,
Moderne Herrn des Zinses und der Arbeit.

Mit Namen tief gekerbt in Marmorstein,
Gehört ihnen allein der Pseudo-Tempel,
Der eiserne Akanthus und das Schullatein,
Die Buchsbaumhecke und die Vögelein.

Und noch im Tode drängen sich die Armen,
Intim gepfercht zwischen den schmalen Pfaden,
Unter den einförmigen Rohsteinplatten,
Den synonymen Kreuzen der Fabrik.

Ja, auch im Tode sind die Städte ungeplant.
Die Erben herrschen aus den alten Zentren,
Sie weichen nicht. Die lächerlichen Englein,
Reste der Armen, fliegen nimmer auf,
Vermehren sich bloss, wie eh und je, im Gras.

He wrote from New Guinea that reading it made him feel he was traveling in a foreign country.

By the time we received *V-Letter*, the book, inscribed by Karl, he was on his way home, and was the American Poet of the Hour. Evalyn had represented him so well in New York that she was elected a member of the Poetry Society in her own right. They were married soon after his return, and we saw them again for the first time in years at a publisher's party for Karl, Arthur Miller (for his novel, *Focus*) and David Cornel de Jong, from which we drove them home to the rented Robert Coates house in Gaylordsville, Ct. The four of us saw the first production of Eliot's *The Cocktail Party* together, a year or two afterward. The last time I saw them together was after my marriage had ended and I was passing through Chicago, when Karl was at *Poetry* magazine. They had three children, had not aged by anything like the twelve years that had passed since our

*See p. 52 for the original of this poem.

first time, and were a glamorous, famous couple, in the late summer of 1954. Their marriage was to last another eleven years or so. By this time Alvin had gone from Freud to Wilhelm Reich, and I remember Reich saying that five years is about as long as a marriage can keep from going stale, so by that criterion we all did well enough.

After the visit to Chicago, our correspondence picked up briefly, and by coincidence my last letter from Karl, in October 1954, begins: "Maybe this will be the first letter to reach your new home. If so, it will be a kind of welcome ..." I had just moved with my two sons to my present apartment in Manhattan, which is where Karl and I live today.

We had been completely out of touch for nearly thirty years when I cam across an interview given by Karl in *The American Poetry Review*, given me by my friend and neighbor Babette Deutsch who had been among his earliest admirers in the poets' world, so we often spoke of him and his poems. It brought the past so vividly to mind. Also, I was feeling particularly isolated that year, immersed since 1979 in the translation of Robert Musil's *The Man Without Qualities* in four volumes, for Knopf, no end in sight. So I impulsively wrote a letter to Karl, like someone waving in order not to drown, I suppose. This was in August, 1982, and I had no knowledge of his second marriage nor that it had ended, with his wife's death, in July 1982. Nor did I send the letter, having no reason to suppose that he would even remember me at all, while his poems and his advancing career had kept me vividly aware of him all along. But the letter turned up among my papers in November, all stamped and ready to mail, and so I decided not to waste it, and phoned to check the address, and accidentally roused Karl from sleep at 6 a m on a Sunday morning, having been oblivious to the time difference (never telephoned California before). When I apologetically identified myself, he insisted that he remembered me very well, and gave me the new address. This time the correspondence had much backlog to flourish on. In early March 1983 he came to New York for a week between terms—still teaching at UCD—and we met every day. I had gotten him a suite at the *Mayflower Hotel* on Central Park West, where Thomas Mann once stayed, with a view of the park, so that the poet who had once written, in *The Bourgeois Poet*:

New York, my love, we never went to bed. (You never asked me.)

could at least go to bed with Central Park. And I put some huge chrysanthemums on his coffee table to greet him on arrival. They prompted the following poem, which eventually appeared in The New Yorker:

The Spider Mums

The spider mums are yellow
In the chill green room.
Six days from the florist
And standing center stage—
How well they hold their age!

Crystals dropped in water
Perpetuate the bloom
Like Stendhal's twigs of diamonds
Created overnight
Of ancient salt and light.

Essays on time get nowhere
But back where they began.
Still, crystallization
Can be the first in art
Though permanent flowers aren't.

Again I was granted that privileged insight into the marvel of metamorphosis, life into art, when realities normally apprehended in the scattered, fleeting way we do are captured, intensified by transposition, raised to a higher power, endowed with significance and sometimes enduring life, at least saved from oblivion. Karl did it again with, among other things, New York scenes so familiar they had virtually ceased to exist, as in "Grant's Tomb Revisited," "The Cathedral Bells," "Girls Fighting, Broadway," and some not yet published, like "The Cloisters." Here it is in part:

Yesterday we took the bus to the Cloisters,
Sixty blocks of black and hispanic slums,

The borough of the Underclass,
Streets and sidewalks mobbed with Harlemites
And one Jew in a round black hat and beard.

Suddenly we drop five hundred years in time,
Stand in a monastery in hushed stone rooms,
Eyeballing saints and virgins and altar pieces
And Bavarian candlesticks seven feet high.
We are the dwarfs of time.
                               In the carven atrium
White cyclamens are blindingly blooming,
And a hundred herbs from Columbus's time.
These cloisters too are Rockefeller, and also Whitman.

Where I sit and do my writing
Two giant cathedrals form the barrier
Between the third world and whatever world ours is.
The Cloisters remind us of return,
The Cloisters imported stone by stone from time,
From Romanesque to Columbus' time to us,
The Cloisters wait for us with outstretched arms,
Even with "wheelchair accessibility."

    I had been to the Cloisters so many times over so many years. They had been a refuge, an oasis of serenity, beauty, recovery, soon undone by the rigors and ugly noise of the return journey. With the poem, they are mine with a kind of reassuring constancy, repossessed every time in the pleasurable journey of perusing it, married to time and place, secure on the map of love.

    Why do women flock to poets, anyway? It's not only their beautiful eyes, beautiful eyes are a dime a dozen. My guess is that women crave attention, discriminating, subtle, compelling, indistractible attention, they can't get enough of it, and hardly ever do. And poets are second only to painters, if at all, in being understood to pay attention and being the cause that this kind of discriminating (in the good sense) attention is paid. Discriminating and constructive in the sense that something is created in the poetic process which enriches the raw material with meaning purpose life it did not have before it received the poet's attention. Is this why Oscar Wilde said "A man can live three days without water but not one without poetry?" Or was he just being candid about his outsized narcissism which demands undeviating attention to oneself. Ah, that's the rub, for naive attention-seekers.

But I seem to have sidetracked myself, out of despair at not having even begun to do justice to KS and his special magic. There is only the hope that a few sparks have been thrown off, like the mating signals of lightning-bugs, enough to attract the attention of some *miglior fabbro* who can do it better.

KARL SHAPIRO

"SPINNING OUT PHOTO-CIRCULARS OF LIGHT"

Norfolk, Va. About 1918. Left to right: Karl, Sarah (Mother), Margery, Irwin

"But he who reads thinks..."

Baltimore, 1941

"And the peace is made fast on the earth and the earth is made fair"

Sydney, Australia, 1942

"Good poetry gives man pause,
Exemplifies the quest, suggests a goal;
Great art legitimizes man."

John Hopkins Professor, about 1948

"It would be like him to say, how many times and ways,
I loathe *poetry*,
Leaving the reader to decide what he meant by poetry
Which he defined, how many times and ways,
Or what he meant by *loathe*,
Or simply what he meant at all.
Or as he had his lady say,
That is not what I meant, at all.
That's what he meant, precisely,
The meaning of *meant*."

With T.S. Eliot at a party, Poetry offices, Chicago

"What shall I teach in the vivid afternoon ..."

Cherry blossoms in Washington, D.C.

"Real speech, real life are unwritten. Only these lines have a tendency to remain forever. Cities with poetry remember him. Cities without poetry."

"Behind me rears my wall of books …"

Karl Shapiro, 1979

"Where thoughts sip peace and garden..."

"I dreamed I held a poem and knew . . ."

~*KS*~

Karl Shapiro

NOTES ON RAISING A POET

I begin with an Auden Thanksgiving. This was one of his last poems.

A THANKSGIVING

When pre-pubescent I felt
that moorlands and woodlands were sacred:
people seemed rather profane.

Thus, when I started to verse,
I presently sat at the feet of
Hardy and *Thomas* and *Frost*.

Falling in love altered that,
now Someone, at least, was important:
Yeats was a help, so was *Graves*.

Then, without warning, the whole
Economy suddenly crumbled;
there, to instruct me, was *Brecht*.

Finally, hair-raising things
that Hitler and Stalin were doing
forced me to think about God.

Why was I sure they were wrong?
Wild *Kierkegaard, Williams* and *Lewis*
guided me back to belief.

Now, as I mellow in years
and home in a bountiful landscape,
Nature allures me again.

Who are the tutors I need?
Well, *Horace,* adroitest of makers,
beeking in Tivoli, and

*Reading given at the New York Historical Society on December 3, 1990.

Goethe, devoted to stones,
who guessed that—he never could prove it—
Newton led Science astray.

Fondly I ponder You all:
without You I couldn't have managed
even my weakest of lines.

? May 1973

I should mention that Thomas is Edward, Williams is Charles, and Lewis is C.S.

***

If there is any heaven for poets, Auden will be in it. T.S. Eliot will be in it of course, as an usher probably. Frequently Eliot will visit the Manager to try to persuade Him to release his mentor Pound from the Waiting-Room. The Manager is always non-committal. Eliot suspects that the Manager is from New York.

We should remember that Auden wrote, I am a New Yorker, not an American. I take this to be a key. For instance I live in New York part of each year but say, I am an American, not a New Yorker.

When I was a sophomore in college and heard that Auden was moving to the United States permanently, I wrote him a long sophomoric letter in which I hoped he would not settle in New England. Too much like Old England I said. Auden replied with a postcard which said Thank you very much. But I've always wondered whether I put a bee in his bonnet.

I've written several poems to Auden, my latest being an elegy in which I claim that he is the poet who made poetry whole again. In the process he put a stop to the Modern. So wide was his perspective that he could situate the Modern as a moment in literary time. The influence of Eliot and Pound stops with Auden; if it survives at all it is by way of William Carlos Williams. My generation of poets, almost to a man or woman, are Auden babies. This means that we eschewed the technique of disjecta membra and set about to put Humpty-Dumpty back together again. Our logo might have been Make It Whole, following Auden's passion for unity and tidiness. For Eliot's dissociation of sensibility and theological pessimism we supplied a humanistic meliorism and still do—what is left of us. I will call the roll shortly.

***

James Merrill speaking in this program a couple of years ago adduced Rilke as a god in our pantheon. Rilke is one of the high magnitude stars in our constellation. It is Rilke's intellectual sensuality that reaches us, much as Lawrence does in his Birds, Beasts and Flowers. Lawrence is a star of lesser magnitude in our pantheon. Baudelaire is a big star, unless, as I sometimes fear, that he is the black hole in our constellation. No poet of our generation has escaped the attraction of Baudelaire. One way to exorcise him is to translate him. I translated two of his sonnets on a troopship, an ideal setting for translating Baudelaire. As soldiers in the First World War supposedly carried Homer into the trenches, so I imagine each American poet carrying his Les Fleurs du Mal in the second.. I carried two copies, a French edition and a bilingual.

***

In his Thanksgiving poem Auden juxtaposes literary influence and ideology. Nature worship leads to Hardy and Frost, and people are "rather profane." Falling in love as a corrective evokes Yeats. But economic collapse is a corrective to love, in Auden's conscience. Love is now "criminal" says Auden in one of his richest (and suppressed) poems, "The Malverns." Enter Karl Marx. Auden now begins to write propaganda, my generation following him at every step. Randall Jarrell is so bewitched by Auden that he will spend years writing a book trying to destroy him. The book is never quite finished. At length the shadow of Hitler's war brings the poet back to God. Kierkegaard, Charles Williams and Screwtape Lewis assist at the rechristening of Auden. But the threat of war drives Auden to America, a move which the British never forgive him for. Exit Karl Marx. (In New Guinea in uniform I am also involved in becoming a Christian, a Roman Catholic in fact, but cannot interest the priest-chaplain that I visit to take on my case.)

***

Auden's thanksgiving poem skips the American experience altogether. He is after all an unreconstructed European. In one of my Auden poems I say he camped out in America. It is a jaunty sonnet that goes:

Without him many of us would never have happened
But would have gone on being Georgians or worse;
We all recalled how he galloped into verse
On Skelton's nag and easily reopened

Eighteenth century prosody like a can of worms,
And there like Alice on a checkerboard
Careened through Marx and Freud and Kierkegaard
Dazzled and dazzling all the ideas and forms,

And camped out in the United States to wrinkle
Like an Indian squaw to await the Nobel Prize
And study savages with paleface eyes
And sit on Oxford dictionaries and rankle.

God bless this poet who took the honest chances;
God bless the live poets whom his art enhances.

At the end, in his bountiful Austrian landscape Auden finally feels at home and writes under the aegis of Horace and Goethe. Unlike most critics I believe that Auden's Kirchstetten poems are among his finest.

***

The tone of voice of poetry in our time is the tone of voice of talk. This is no age for epics. Any attempt at the grand form ends in embarrassing parody, like the schizophrenic spiderweb of the Cantos or the quixotic omnium gatherum of The Bridge. The closest we can get to epic is in the interior monody such as The Duino Elegies or the Four Quartets. Nor can poetry in our age of prose reach for the footlights except in the conversational livingroom tone of voice. From the pulpit to the oval office to the poet's podium we have lost elevated language. Such was the honest instruction of Hardy and Frost. And of course since speech is the touchstone of our poetics we might have expected poetry to sink down to the mire as well, and thus we are treated today to the poetry of muck, as never before in literary history. Of course there is little chance that any of it will survive. Even Auden wrote his porno poem called, if I remember, "The Platonic Blow." Vulgarity in Auden however is a tour de force. Megalopolis was not good for Auden. Poems like "City Without Walls" and "The Shield of Achilles" are heart breakers in urban poetry. I published "The Shield of Achilles" in *Poetry Magazine* and gave it our best prize. It was as if the Just City was gone forever.

***

Auden's most famous—and silliest—critical remark was that poetry makes nothing happen. In contradicting Shelley's equally silly remark about Unacknowledged Legislators Auden was just stamping his foot. Auden made a whole generation of poets happen. And best of all, poetry made Auden happen.

***

Because poetry in our time has become increasingly ideological, it has had to steer between many dangerous rocks and shoals. Have we really navigated between the Scylla of Marxism and the Charybdis of Freudianism? Has Marxism really foundered or is it just snorkling? And what about Freud and his Ism? Has the head shrinker finally become the shrunken head? We can only hope for the best.

***

It is as if poetry in the academy, where it is now roosting, is beset by every variety of enemy. The ideologues are after us! yells the poet, scrambling away from the latest Structuralist and his hydrophobic half-brother called Deconstruction. Strange fighting words assail us: French, which supplies the world with military terminology, gives us the linguistic weapon *découpage*. I consult the dictionary. *Découper* means to cut into pieces, to cut up, to pink, to slash, to cut out, to punch. And what is being cut into pieces, picked, slashed and punched? Why, *le texte* of course. To be sure, le texte doesn't refer to poetry or fiction alone. Le texte can refer to "any cultural product." These fellows leave no stone standing.

***

You know Henry James' quip about Walt Whitman, that Whitman knew too many languages. His camerados, his eleves, his eidolons are benchmarks of his style. He hadn't caught on to Black Pidgin—he left that to John Berryman. Or to Yiddish-American—he left that to Saul Bellow. Or even to plain American which even cats and dogs can read. He left that to Randall Jarrell and surprisingly to Auden and I might add "hopefully" to me. Whitman remains the pole star of our poetry and yet he is embattled today as in his lifetime. Let's not get into that. Instead I will read my Whitman poem:

WHITMAN

Like Queen Victoria, he used the regal *we*,
Meaning the disciples of *Leaves of Grass*,
The American Bible, they literally believed;
Sat by the hour to photographers,
The Open Shirt frontispiece,
The Good Gray, the Jesus, the Laughing Philosopher,
The Old Poet in the crumpled highcrown hat
Gazing in rapture at the butterfly
   Perched on his forefinger
(It turns out was a cardboard butterfly);
To Tennyson the greatest of his time,
Inviting Walt to sail to the Isle of Wight;
Our first and probably our only guru,
Whose opinion of niggers (his designation) was low,
But worshipped Lincoln to whom he scribed
   His second greatest song;
Who opened the Closet but wouldn't come out;
Who lived in a kind of luxurious poverty,
Housekeeper, male nurse, amanuensis, carriage,
   On the bounty of admirers,
Adored as Gandhi or a Dr. Schweitzer,
Visited by Oscar Wilde and English titles,
   In Camden, New Jersey;
Two hundred pounds of genius and hype,
Nature-mystic who designed his tomb
Solid as an Egyptian pyramid,
American to the soles of his boots,
Outspoken as Christ or Madame Blavatsky,
Messiah, Muse of the Modern, Mother!

***

We can smile at the polyglot Whitman and groan at the polyglot Pound. Language has always been the central problem of our poetry; anxiety of identity is the peculiar American worry. Sometimes we hang onto English in a panic. I am a member of a lobby called U.S. English. In fact I am on board with Jacques Barzun, Saul Bellow and Arnold Schwartzenegger. We are trying to make English the official language of the United States. At last count we have already garnered nineteen states. I am stuck with a dichotomy. As a poet I believe in the language stew. As a professor of poetry and an American I believe in a normative English to stave off linguistic anarchy. There is no point trying to reconcile the two positions. There is no reconciliation. A language history tells me that English began as a lowly German dialect. It is "a language that succeeded almost by stealth, treated for centuries as the inadequate and second-rate tongue of peasants...(yet) it has become the most important and successful language in the world." With the help of the Romans and the French, to be sure. The international character of English began only a generation after Shakespeare, when the language was exported to the New World. English today is an American export.

The latest tsunami of immigration, legal and otherwise, threatens the domination of English for the first time since the early days of the Colonies, when it appeared that French or even German might become the national tongue. I have just received an advertisement from my telephone company in California which is printed in English, Spanish, Portuguese and according to my count *twelve* Oriental languages. The immediate threat is from the Hispanic sector which has already made serious inroads in the schools. We fight this as best we can. In my English Department in California I fought against the institution of Black English as well. We are in a linguistic Civil War.

***

My first poetry teacher was my brother, though he wasn't aware of it. He was a wunderkind, a year older than me. At sixteen he had already won a four-year scholarship to the University of Virginia, and won the state poetry contest for a poem he read on the famous campus, family attending. The poem was in Imagist style, a new and controversial technique at the time. The University of Virginia is a sacred place in my psyche, though I wrote a wicked poem about it when I dropped out of there in my freshman year. Teaching in the Virginia public schools was rigorous in the Twenties. We drilled in Latin, French, grammatical English and versification. There was massive memorization, still the best training for poetry ever devised. Surprisingly, beside the Chaucer and Shakespeare and the Romantics we were introduced to the contemporaries Eliot, Lindsay, Amy Lowell. I do not recall any Pound. Nor do I remember, in our anthology called Southern Prose and Poetry, any Faulkner.

When Thomas Jefferson was planning his famous university he outlined his curriculum. I mention the language requirements only. And this was for beginners. Ancient languages: Greek, Latin, Hebrew. Modern languages: French, Italian, German, Spanish, Anglo-Saxon. Over a century later when I matriculated at the university, little if any of this was required. The year I graduated from high school, 1932, was the last year classical Greek was taught. I stole a library copy of the Odes of Anacreon which I could not read and a rhyming dictionary with an introduction by George Saintsbury. I learned rhyming from Saintsbury. At the University I learned enough Greek to read Plato and the New Testament, which my professor called baby Greek. I was astonished when I taught at the University of Nebraska to discover that students of dentistry were required to take a course in Greek, though literature students were not. Dental Greek? Of course, so they could understand the difficult terminology of their science. I know that a lot of my vocabulary and even syntax in my poems comes from the Latin I once knew well. In Modern languages we avoided German because after the First World War German was no longer taught. It was, like Versailles, part of the punishment. In Baltimore where I lived even a street named German Street was renamed Redwood Street. I regret not knowing my parent language. My contemporary Randall Jarrell fell in love with German and played with it in his poetry. But today I look at the students and think, if only they could learn English!

How language, literature and poetry training turned into Creative Writing I will leave to the sociologists. But let me read my poem called Creative Writing.

Karl Shapiro

CREATIVE WRITING

English was in its autumn when this weed
Sprang up on every quad.
The Humanities had long since gone to seed,
Grammar and prosody were as dead as Aztec.
Everyone was antsy except the Deans
Who smelled Innovation, Creativity!
Even athletes could take Creative Writing:
No books, no tests, best grades guaranteed,
A built-in therapy for all and sundry,
Taking in each other's laundry.
No schedule, no syllabus, no curriculum,
No more reading; knowledge has gone elsewhere.
Pry yourself open with a speculum
And put a tangle in your hair.

It spread from graduate school to kindergarten,
It moved to prisons, to aircraft carriers,
Competing with movies, blackjack and craps.
Civil war flared up from time to time
When pure professors decided to weed the Grove,
Insecticide the pest, but the creative seed,
Stronger than gonorrhea or the med-fly,
Bounced down the highways like a tumbleweed,
Took to the air and the ocean seas,
Mated in Paris with the Fleur-de-lys.

When I heard that one of my creative writing students had gotten a job teaching it on an aircraft carrier I was ready to cheer. Such an act of humanity, never mind how zany must be its own reward. My ex-student was a Vietnam veteran, badly damaged by drugs but now doing heroic service on the high seas. Maybe Creative Writing was a form of damage control? In any case it was by now universal in the education world and the name was part of the language. What was the point of my ranting? Toward the end of my teaching career I was asked to give a faculty lecture and delivered a talk called Creative Glut in which I berated Humanities

Departments for intellectual cowardice and English Departments in particular for pandering to the mindless panhandling of the Creative lobby. Not that my lecture made any difference, except to make my colleagues look at me sidewise.

For someone who has made a comfortable living all his adult life teaching Creative Writing it would seem irrational and wrong-headed to oppose it. If CW is no more than what lawyers call a good faith effort to help writers and poets have a job, that would be enough to justify it. Why shouldn't poets have a job, even if they only have to lean on their shovels? I only wish that Creative Writing would not be confused with education, that it would not try to compete with language and literature training as an equal. But it does. It even supersedes them. In a recent issue of AWP (Associated Writing Programs, a lobby for Creative Writing) I read that academic degrees should not be required of writers but that "parity" should be established in the matter of salaries and that the MFA degree, where required, should be considered the equivalent of the Ph.D. in literature, linguistics or composition. Simultaneously, course loads for writers or poets should be reduced to a minimum, so as not to interfere with the Muse. This massive boondoggle is taken seriously. In this era of catatonic artist-worship the writer or artist gets whatever he asks for, the tax-paying public be damned.

Polemics aside, do these Creative Writing programs achieve what they claim? Are we in a poetic Renaissance? Has American poetry swept the world, the way the English language has? Let us glance at the results of half a century of Creative Writing.

***

Taking 1940 as a guesswork starting point of CW, when only the U. of Iowa was engaging in the pursuit (I dropped out of their faculty too), I offer these comparisons. In 1940 there were only about a half dozen literary magazines of any account and only about a dozen poets so recognized. In 1990 there are at least a thousand literary magazines, *soi-disant,* and the population of poets is so large that one poetry lobby publishes a large directory giving names and addresses and even phone numbers of the poets. In the 1940's a poet could not get a university job unless he was an English professor. In the 1990's having an English professor title would be held against him; it would suggest a certain impurity. (I should say that in the late Forties I was hired as an Associate Professor of English at John Hopkins with tenure, but quit after three years, so I must have been an entering wedge of some kind. I had no degrees of any kind but had won some appropriate prizes. I had also given a try-out lecture which impressed the English professors and philologists. The subject was classical English prosody in transition.) Again, in the Forties poetry readings were rare to unknown. Today there are as many poetry readings as there are poets. Public ventilation is part of the new role of the poet. Public entertainment, frequently in bars and night clubs, is more like it. Po-Biz as it is called is only a variant of Sho-Biz. The atmosphere is conducive to sexual language, the use of which in 1940 would and did send author, publisher and bookseller to jail. (A couple of years ago I also read in a Greenwich Village nightclub. I read a long unpublished poem called "Fucking." It was a serious poem about the misuse of the word and its act.) Also in self-defense, as I am basically prudish about language, I should say that I am the author of the introduction to Tropic of Cancer which helped clear that book for American publication. But I still make the old-fashioned distinction between literature and life. Finally, book publication was rare for poets in the Forties. Today poetry books, chapbooks and recordings are universal. Big publishers have not changed, of course, and are as suspicious and inhospitable to poetry as always. On the other hand, universities almost en bloc publish, much of it the best going. Altogether poetry has ceased to be hermetic. And poets constitute a new social grouping, with their own manners, dress and what journalists call life-style. One sometimes suspects that this new confederation of poets operates by a Code which includes politics, religion and esthetic guidelines. There is an alarming uniformity. One hears the expression Creative Clones and the reference to their product as the McPoem.

**

There has been much writing about the split American heritage, the struggle between the Old Adam and the New Adam. The old Adam is the destructive, disintegrative force exemplified in poets like Poe and Pound and Eliot. D.H. Lawrence wrote a famous book of essays along these lines. The new Adam in our time blossoms in the parking lot poems of William Carlos Williams, those prescription pad poems which are among the best the 20th century has produced. Here is a new poem about WCW.

BILL WILLIAMS

It's the woman in me that writes poetry, said Bill,
    Who was not even homosexual (we think)
But was gay in the time-honored sense,
    O happy paradox, a happy poet,
Hard-working slum doc and fulltime poet
    Whose poems were prescription,
Who tried to get the monkey Ezra off his back
    And never quite kicked the habit,
Who hated the Possum with a hate that was more than hate,
Archbishop Possum who flicked him away like a bug
    and went on butlering English verse.
Talk about the pure products of America going crazy,
    Doc Williams was crazy with sanity.

Williams was homespun. Pound faked his Americanism and couldn't bring it off. I find that the best way to deal with Pound is in doggerel:

A DOGGEREL FOR EZRA

Pound came on the heels of Joaquin "Murieta" Miller,
The latest American buffoon to pass himself off
    in the Empire of Brit
    as frontiersman and poet
    in his cape and cowhide boots,
Sealskin coat, red shirt and Stetson hat,
Plus the obligatory beard and hair.
Pound simplified the disguise
    to cape, sombrero and beard

And set up shop to issue manifests in London.

He was born in the territory of the Aryan brotherhood
Who think it's their responsibility to purify the blood.
He was only a graduate student with an evangelistic gleam;
To carry culture to the West was his obsessive dream.
His bible was a booklist that he himself compiled,
A list to save the mind and soul of every Yanky child.
He was hell-bent on the Modern language of here-and-now
But he couldn't get rid of the antique biblical use of thou,
He messed around incessantly with other poet's pages,
Eliot, Propertius, Kung Fu, scholars and poets and sages.
He became the poet of money, a funny thing to doo
For one who blamed all evils on the money-hungry Jew.
He messed around with his opus and ultimately confessed
He didn't know where it was going, no matter how much he messed.
But he left a prosodic testament, his real and only will,
To a poet back in New Jersey who liked to be called Just Bill.

***

I include Constantine Cavafy in our constellation, a special luminary. Auden wrote an introduction to Cavafy's poems, even though Auden didn't read Cavafy's modern Greek, much less the demotic that Cavafy stirred into his idiom. It is certainly a mark of a certain greatness that his poetry overleaps the language barriers. Auden freely admits the Greek poet's influence on him. At least one poem of Auden's, "Atlantis," is practically a steal from Cavafy's "Ithaca." Cavafy is a strange mixture of the erotic, in the Greek sense, and the historical. He is an interpreter of Hellenistic myth and culture, that crossroads of religion and civilization, with its powerful odor of decadence. Cavafy helps Europeanize the term Modern, as Auden does. His poem "Waiting for the Barbarians" has become almost a themesong of Modernity.

G.M. Hopkins is also a very high magnitude star in our constellation, in many way the godfather of the Modern, apropos of poetry and our language.

GERARD MANLEY HOPKINS MESMERIZES A DUCK

It's his own description. You can look it up.
Hopkins held a duck's head down on a table
    And drew a chalk line at the beak;
Removed his hand and the duck was mesmerized;
Erased the line and the duck got up.
Association of the hand and the line
    The experts said.
Fascinating instress of the straight white stroke
    The poet replied.

Oh that mythical desert island where the sole survivor
    Is allowed only one book
I, castaway of the three-score-ten, and some,
    Have made my selection:
Neither the Bible nor Shakespeare not the aidful
    Do-it-yourself *Robinson Crusoe*
But a paperback Penguin bearing the beautiful name
    Gerard Manley Hopkins
Which he thought was such a funny name
He wanted to change it, mirabile dictu,
    To Pook Tuncks.

Philosopher who ditched the Stagirite
    In favor of the Dunce,
Who admired Walt and called him a great scoundrel,
Remained step-poet embalmed and treasured up
    By Bridges, dulcet Dixon, Patmore,
More patiently awaiting exhumation,
One of the Lesser Greaters we now know,
    And too will times to come and times to come.

    I quote a startling observation of the critic and scholar Wallace Fowlie. In the 19th century, Fowlie says, one could take a blind man to the play and he would follow and understand the whole piece. In the 20th century one can seat a deaf man in front of a television play and he will understand the whole piece. What has happened? Language is lost. We communicate by pictures in an eerie light. There is something subconscious about television light and computer light. Is it some kind of twilight of the mind? Does poetry also express this dissolution of language? I hear a new expression from the disaffected sector of poets: Language Poets. Is that a term of derision? Are they talking about poetry *without* language? Reading a lot of contemporary verse I sometimes think that that is their goal.

***

Psychological and political theories and fads have always beset the artist, who has constantly to be aware of the trip-wires and booby-traps of critics and intellectuals. The popular ideologies are at present comatose: Marxism and Freudianism have had it. Linguistic kibitzers have taken their place and continue to poke and prod the poetic psychic wound. The freudian idea that art was a form of mental illness has been supplanted by the linguistic notion that art is a form of fraud. This keeps the creative writing classes in a state of almost joyous anxiety.

***

Social levelling carries a high cost. In one of my Creative Writing classes a student said to me that he objected to my use of the word classics. You have your classics he said; we have ours, though he didn't name any. This erasure of qualitative distinctions denies a fixity of standards. If there are no landmarks, no milestone, no points of reference, no models, then we are set adrift, rudderless. The fifty or sixty thousand books published annually in this country reflect this anarchy. I recall attending a lecture on my campus by William F. Buckley; there were over two thousand students in the audience. They sat in a silence such as I never heard. Not that they agreed or disagreed with what they heard. I doubt if more than a handful understood his sentences. I think they were stunned by the experience of hearing an American speak advanced English.

***

A couple of years ago the critic Joseph Epstein published an article called Who Killed Poetry? The outcry from the poetry establishments was little short of thunderous. Organized poetry answered the call to arms.

Then it all died down and everything returned to the status quo ante. But Epstein had touched a raw nerve, arguing somewhat along the lines of my own observations. He quotes a remark of Kingsley Amis which sums up the whole case. "Everything that has gone wrong since World War II can be summed up in the word — "workshop." Does this mean that history, literature, even poetry are, since the War, run and operated by committee? Creative Writing is certainly writing by committee. That's what those messy sessions are about. But of course Epstein's banner title was meant to provoke and alarm. What disturbs him and people like me is not that poetry is dead but that it is running wild. It's no accident that the poetry wildfire coincides with the generation that tried and almost succeeded in burning the schoolhouse down, the generation of sexual tohu va bohu, of Ho Chee Min, Ginsberg and Leary, porn for all, the generation of the slogan "Everything is political"—because the poetry wildfire is exactly that—political. Epstein's article points out that it is the generation of the Sixties that now provides the tenured professors in all the colleges and universities of the land and who are the guardians of the Creative Writing dens. It may be another generation or two before the Humanities regain their footing. I was pleased to notice that several of my own Creative Writers decided to work towards the Ph.D., finding that their minds were unfurnished.

There is indeed a widespread withdrawal from poetry in this country, amounting almost to a boycott. Literate people hope the wildfire will burn itself out, that the university will come to its senses. Lined up against the Levelers and their bureaucratic colleagues are a few small but telling pockets of resistance. One hysteric leveller refers to Allen Bloom, Saul Bellow and William Bennet as The Killer B's. Childish epithets are hurled: elitist, reactionary, even fascist. I was called fascist-in-residence when I opposed the levellers in my department.

Here is a poem by William Jay Smith called "The Tall Poets," a piece of work which I think ranks up there with Prufrock. It is the kind of poem which makes me say, I wish I had written that.

Karl Shapiro

THE TALL POETS

A Bicentennial Meditation—July 4, 1976

While the sky above Manhattan flaps with a thousand Jasper Johns,
past file after file of duplicate jubilant faces—
under the glorious gray-green artichoke crown of Liberty,
their free-flowing purple beards catching fire in the morning light
and trailing behind them in wondrous ash-blue wakes
on the welcoming water,
the Tall Poets—in Operation Poetry—
sail up the lordly Hudson.

Manned by the Irish Mafia and the Jewish Mafia
and the Yugoslavian Mafia
(whatever happened to the Sicilian Mafia?)—
a light breeze rippling the fluent free verse of their rigging—
together with the Tall Women Poets,
decked out in tough companionate canvas pants suits,
vulvas cleaving the wind,
the Tall Poets proceed pontifically up the lordly Hudson
on this bright Bicentennial morning.

And there in the mid-Mondrian of Manhattan—
with the boogie-woogie beat of its red white and blue squares—
beside her jade plant and her rubber plant and her Kaffir lily,
beside her innumerable cascading spider plants,
in her Empire chair
beside her Louis Seize commode—
my lady, the lovely long-legged Swan of Strasbourg,
(Yes, Lafayette, she is here)
leans this morning from her white air-conditioned tower,
brooding over the gray water, and she says:
"Where are you, William, why are you not here,
your blue beard billowing above the water,
your majestic *vers libre* ribboning out on the wind—
why are you not here sailing among the Tallest of the Tall Poets—
in Operation Poetry—
up the lordly Hudson?
Why do you dither down there in your dark bayou?

Why do you not let it all hang out
on this bright Bicentennial morning?")

So speaks my beloved, the Swan of Strasbourg,
and I look northward toward her white air-conditioned tower,
and wiping my forehead in the steaming swamp, I answer:
"O my Swan, I wish that I could join you there
in that bright and bugling Bicentennial air—
but my beard, my love,
(the legacy of my Choctaw forebears)
grows solely on my lips and chin
and when it grows I look like Ho Chi Minh
(or did when I was thin)
but now under the TV cameras
my eyebrows disappear—and my beard
becomes a wreath of cobwebs
around a moon-shaped face
until I look like the ghost of Mao Tse-Tung ...
How wretched and ridiculous I would appear,
sailing up the lordly Hudson there
on this bright Bicentennial morning ...

"And besides, I am bored with those Tall Poets,
those first and second generation baby Bunyans,
sick of their creatively written writing,
their blithering buffoonery, their diapered Dada,
their petulant pornography,
their syrupy self-pitying self-interviews,
their admired ash-buried academic anorexia ...
I'm weary of having to dive into their driven dreck that hits the fan
weekly in every puffed and pompous periodical....
I long for the pure poem,
the passionate statement,
the simple declarative sentence ...
We live in a bad time ... and I cannot write ...
I paddle around this black bayou in my pirogue...
Spanish moss hangs from the live oaks like the smoke of innumerable
                cigarettes,
and the cypress knees protrude from the black water

like arthritic fingers above a silent typewriter keyboard....
In the dead silence of the bayou a voice deep within me says:
'Walt Whitman is alive and well, and inhabits the Bronx;
he teaches at Stony Brook, and knows exactly what America is
    thinking.
To hell with rhyme and reason, Walt, unwind ... Poor Smith is a
    hack
overly enamored of writer's block:
he doesn't even know what he thinks until he's said
it; and he has nothing to say.
His mind is as blank as the wobbly whiskered wall-eyed catfish
that he pulled out of the bayou
on this bright Bicentennial morning.'
So says the inner voice while light creaks
down through the rose windows of the cypresses,
and a woodpecker pecks on the dead wood overhead."

From her white air-conditioned tower the Swan of Strasbourg speaks:
"Don't be silly. Stop paddling around in your little pirogue.
Get out of the black backwater of that bayou:
come back up here to the lordly Hudson,
and be the Tall Poet God intended you to be.
Join the other Tall Poets.
Magne-toi le popotin! I didn't marry a piddling paddler of pirogues!"

"Swan," I say, "I know that your great-uncle designed those broad
    avenues in Paris,
and where would we be, I hesitate to say,
without the Champs Elysées?
But I don't feel a bit monumental this Bicentennial morning ...
Come down, my darling, from your white tower; leave your
Louis Seize commode
and your Empire chair and your *Compagnie des Indes* china
behind you: come down here to join me in my pirogue,
and together we shall thread our way through the innumerable
Louisiana bayous
as intricate as the branches of your spider plants ...
through the land of my birth ... past Dugdemona Swamp and Saline
    Lake—

past the *Cote joyeuse* and down the Red River like my forebears
past the bearded oaks and the sagging white columns of the plantations
and the writhing black grillwork of Bourbon Street ...
through the jubilant notes of early jazz ...
and finally out into the glorious Gulf ... and the light around us will be pale green—
feathery and fine as stalks of fennel against a background
    of mother-of-pearl,
and when we reach a point unknown on any chart,
and I can say with your Racine,
'The day is no less pure than the depth of my heart,'
I shall begin to write again; and I shall complete that poem begun
a lifetime ago on the edge of the great brown river
on an April morning beside a bank of violets—
a poem of life and death, of love and memory:

"While the Tall Poets—in Operation Poetry—sail up the lordly
    Hudson,
past the gray contiguous cliffs of the academies,
into the locked and heavily guarded harbors of the anthologies
on this bright Bicentennial morning."

    My generation—those roughly of military age during the Second World War—is a considerable bunch. By and large we were the Auden babies who veered away from Eliot towards Auden, Whitman, Lawrence, Hopkins, Baudelaire and Cavafy. (Notice that there's only one American in that list.) The roll call reads, and this is not complete: Schwartz, Jarrell, Nemerov, William Jay Smith, Elizabeth Bishop, Berryman, Gwendolyn Brooks, Ciardi, James Dickey, Lowell, Meredith, Merrill, Merwin, Nims, Rich, Rukeyser, Simpson, Snodgrass, Stafford, Swenson, Viereck, Galway Kinnell. I count myself in the list. We make a solid anthology. It may or may not be natural for the older generation to look askance at the new one but I believe that we measured ourselves against our models, mostly Europeans by the way, so we expect the younger poets to measure themselves against us. But this does not seem to be the case. It is hard to tell if they have any models or standards at all.

Now after all this complaining I ask myself, What would I do to remedy this state of affairs? How would I go about the upbringing and breeding of poets? My answer is that basically I would do nothing. Poets tend to float and drift and most are autodidacts. On their own they will copy and imitate their elders and betters and will work just as hard adapting to their lessers and inferiors in their demotic environments.

Should poets be in the university and remain there, I ask myself? Not under false pretenses, cheating college, society and themselves. If a poet wishes to undergo the rigors of higher education, fine. If not, he should leave the ivory tower, not treat it like a welfare program. But then, should poets be educated? Answer, that is up to them. A poet can be as educated as Chaucer or as uneducated, we are told, as Shakespeare.

If you were to invent a university curriculum for artists and writers and poets, what would it be like? Instruction in literature taken for granted, a poet's instruction should be in craft only. No theory. Language training would be intensive, poetry in all the original tongues, as in Jefferson's syllabus. We are as you know now living in an age of translation fraudulence., everyone translating from languages they can't read. But preferably poets should learn a trade, medicine, shoe-making, automobile repair, law. Unless they prefer the street,

What about teaching Contemporary Poetry?—It should be outlawed. This is a source of contamination, the backup of sludge. There used to be the idea, I think at Oxbridge, that no writer or artist should be taught until he had been dead a hundred years. Good idea. Of course poets and artists of all kinds should be invited to perform and display their wares on the campus but as guests, never as residents. Unless they belong to the company of scholars.

You are speaking to the Academy of American Poets. What do you want from American poets anyhow? Answer, I once, more than once, wrote an article called Is Poetry an American Art? At the end I made this prescription. (This particular blast is twenty years old but it still sounds like me.)

What would American poetry be like, to deserve the name? Answer: It would be nonsensical, hilarious and obscene like us. Absurd like us. It would be marked as we are by cultural forgetfulness and lack of principle. It would be void of or transvalue all values and ideals, sensual, joyous, bitter, curious, gossipy, knowledgeable to the last minute detail, ungrammatical, endlessly celebrating the facts, objects, neuroses, murders, love affairs and vulgarities of America. Certainly it would develop favorite forms, but these would be soluble in prose. It would be comical and slack and full of junk; impure, generous, bookish and cheap. It would by mystical, savage and drab, and as hateful as Joyce Kilmer's "Trees."

Actually this harangue describes the poetry of Walt Whitman to a T. And all other American poetry tries, though most would deny it, to measure up to *Leaves of Grass*. It can be argued that *The Waste Land* and even the *Cantos* are redactions of *Leaves of Grass*. That work remains as Whitman intended, the Bible of American poetry, blaspheme it as we will.

Auden fled to the New World, to Whitman's island in fact. It was an act of homage.

I began with an Auden Thanksgiving. I will end with an Auden advisory.

W.H. Auden
ODE TO THE MEDIEVAL POETS

Chaucer, Langland, Douglas, Dunbar, with all your
brother Anons, how on earth did you ever manage,
   without anaesthetics or plumbing,
    in daily peril from witches, warlocks.

lepers, The Holy Office, foreign mercenaries
burning as they came, to write so cheerfully,
   with no grimaces of self-pathos?
    Long-winded you could be but not vulgar,

bawdy but not grubby, your raucous flytings
sheer high-spirited fun, whereas our makers,
   beset by every creature comfort,
    immune, they believe, to all superstitions,

even at their best are so often morose or
kinky, petrified by their gorgon egos.
   We all ask, but I doubt if anyone

~ KS ~
Karl Shapiro
VIRGINIA BEACH

In those days blacks didn't go in the ocean
Except at night. You didn't see them then.
How they must have shuddered at the shock
Of the titanic wave that knocked you down.
How they must have shivered on the sand.

It was all mine, the hot and golden beach
All the way from Cape Henry to the North Carolina line
With only a fisherman's shack from mile to mile,
The sharp scrub grass, the dunes, the prickly light.
Alone we dared dive naked through the translucent wave
Crept to the shooting range of the National Guard
Lay close, watching the spatter of machine—
Gun bullets in the sand, seeing how close we could get
Two generations and three wars later
I see a vision of my childhood beach
I never knew, highrise condominiums,
An avenue of boutiques,
Merchandise lying scattered in the streets,
Clothes bunched in the gutter

Sidewalks glittery with fractured glass,
Young men prowling through jagged openings,
Police lights, rifles of the National Guard,
Black men, black men racing towards the dark!

~*KS*~

Sue Walker

DRINKING IRON KUAN YIN WITH KARL SHAPIRO
4/20/91

Even after long storage,
the leaves are like iron
and resist crumbling.
Memory is like that—
this moment with Karl Shapiro.
He is sitting beside me on a beige sofa,
easy in a vest the color of
roses, red outside the window.
The poet, holding a camera in his hands,
looks at me; I am smiling.
The camera captures us:
Connecting our two lives
with strings of words
That you send back this spring
like flights of bird —
a snapshot tucked into a letter.

After dinner, we drink tea bearing the goddess
of mercy's name—Kuan Yin,
talk as leaves steep,
while the teapot itself warms in hot water.
Later, when we say goodby.
Sophie plucks a rose from the garden;
I bring it home, put its petals into potpourri,
and set the pages of this festschrift.
These leaves, Karl, pungent and lasting
as Iron Kuan Yin,
honor you.

NOTES ON CONTRIBUTORS

JOHN BRUGALETTA is a professor of English at California State University, Fullerton, Ca where he is the editor of *South Coast Poetry Journal*. He is the author of two books of poetry, *The Tongue Angles* (Negative Capability Press) and *Tilling The Land* (Mellen Poetry Press.)

HAYDEN CARRUTH is the author of *The Selected Poetry of Hayden Carruth, Mother*, and *Sitting In: Selected Writings on Jazz, the Blues, and Related Topics*. His list of awards includes fellowships from the Bollingen and Guggenheim foundations. Hayden Carruth was Poet-in-Residence at Bucknell University in 1984 and is now a Professor of English at Bucknell University.

LEO CONNELLAN is poet-in-residence at Eastern Connecticut State University. He has published twelve books of poetry, including the widely acclaimed *Clear Blue Lobster-Water Country* and *New And Collected Poems*. His awards include a grant from the National Endowment for the Arts and the Shelley Memorial Award from the Poetry Society of America. Connellan's poems have been recorded by the Library of Congress and he has produced several screen plays. Other volumes of his poetry include *Another Poet in New York, Crossing America, Death in Lobster Land*, and *First Selected Poems*.

ALISTAIR M. DUCKWORTH is a professor of English at the University of Florida, Gainesville, Fl.

LEO HABER works as an editorial consultant for *Midstream*. He is a poet and writer of fiction, having won the 1989 Negative Capability Fiction Award. His work has appeared in *The New York Times, Saturday Review, High Fidelity, Stereo Review, Commentary, Embers, The Literary Review,* and *Ararat*, among others..

JOSEPH HARRIS has published in *America, Hollins Critic, Poetpourri, SD Review, Poet & Critic, Crosscurrents,* and *New Voices*.

TED KOOSER is a poet whose publications include *The Blizzard Voice* (Bieler Press) and *One World At A Time* (University of Pittsburgh Press).

J.T. LEDBETTER is a professor at California Lutheran University. His publications include *Crosscurrents, Puerto Del Sol, The Formalist, Kansas Quarterly,* and *Poetry Review.*

GLENNA LUSCHEI is a poet who is active in the small press community. She has served as Chair of COSMEP and has acted as literature panelist of the NEA. She is the editor of *Cafe Solo* and the author of more than a dozen books, chapbooks, and special editions. She has won the YM-YWHA Poetry Discovery Award and has been awarded both the D.H. Lawrence and Wurlitzer Fellowships in Taos, New Mexico, as well as a National Endowment writer's grant.

JIM LYNCH is an associate professor of English at Orange County Community College, Middletown, NY.

JAMES E. MILLER, JR. is a professor of English at the University of Chicago.

JOHN F. NIMS is the author of *The Six-Cornered Snowflake* (New Directions) and *Zany in Denim* (University of AR. Pres.) He is the editor of *Western Wind: An Introduction to Poetry III,* a text book published by McGraw-Hill.

HANS OSTROM teaches writing and literature at the University of Puget Sound. He is the author of *The Coast Starlight* (Linwood Press), a book of poems that includes an introductory note by Karl Shapiro. Ostrom's poetry, fiction, and reviews have appeared in *Ploughshares, Poetry Northwest, Choice,* and *The San Francisco Chronicle. Lives And Moments: An Introduction To Short Fiction* published by Holt, Rinehart, Winston in 1991.

ROBERT PHILLIPS is the author of *Personal Accounts, Poems 1966-1986.* He is a poet, fiction writer, critic, editor, and anthologist.

LOUIS D. RUBIN, JR. has been executive secretary of the American Studies Association and has taught at Johns Hopkins and Hollins College, and is professor of English at the University of North Carolina at Chapel Hill. He has been awarded Guggenheim and American Council of Learned Societies fellowships, and two of his short stories have appeared in the *Best American Short Stories* collections. He is the editor of the Southern Literary Studies Series of the

Louisiana State University Press. He has published two novels, *The Golden Weather* and *Surfaces of a Diamond*, as well as books on Southern and American literature and history, including *Thomas Wolfe: The Weather of His Youth, No Place on Earth, The Faraway Country, The Curious Death of the Novel, The Wary Fugitives, The Writer in the South, The Teller in the Tale, George W. Cable, William Elliott Shoots a Bear, Virginia: A History, A Gallery of Southerners*, and *The Even-Tempered Angler*. He has been president of the Society for the Study of Southern Literature.

DAVID SLAVITT is a prolific poet, novelist, and translator. Among his recent works are *Lives of the Saints* (Atheneum), *Eight Longer Poems*, and *Equinox* (LSU Press).

JOHN UPDIKE graduated from Harvard College and spent a year in England on the Knox Fellowship at the Ruskin School of Drawing and Fine Art in Oxford. From 1955 to 1957 he was a member of the staff of *The New Yorker*, to which he contributed poems, short stories, essays, and book review. He is the author of fourteen novels. His numerous awards include the Pulitzer Prize, the National Book Award, the American Book Award, and the National Book Critics Circle Award.

PETER VIERECK is a Pulitzer Prize-winning poet and professor of European and Russian history at Mount Holyoke College. He has held an international reputation as an historian, poet, dramatist, and political philosopher. He has received Guggenheim fellowships in poetry as well as history. In 1979 he was appointed to Mount Holyoke's distinguished William R. Kenan, Jr. Chair. His prize-winning books are *Terror & Decorum* (reprinted by Greenwood Press, Westport, CT) and *Archer In The Marrow* (W.W. Norton & Company, New York).

SUE WALKER is a professor of English at the University of South Alabama in Mobile and editor of *Negative Capability*. She is the author of *Traveling My Shadow* and *Shorings* recently published by South Coast Press, California State University, Fullerton.

JOHN WHEATCROFT is the associate editor of *The CEA Critic*, series editor of The Bucknell University Fine Editions books which published *Adam And Eve* by Karl Shapiro. He is a professor of English and Director of the Stadler Center for Poetry at Bucknell University.

SOPHIE WILKINS is a translator and former editor at Knopf.

ACKNOWLEDGMENTS

Grateful acknowledgment is made to the following for permission to reprint previously published material:

LEO CONNELLAN: "Ode to Karl Shapiro" from *New And Collected Poems* by Leo Connellan, Paragon House. Copyright ©1989 by Leo Connellan. Reprinted by permission of the author.

THE ACADEMY OF AMERICAN POETS: "Notes on Raising a Poet" was first given as a lecture entitled "The Education of the Poet" as part of The Academy of American Poets reading series in New York City. Reprinted by permission of The Academy of American Poets.

THE CEA CRITIC: "A Salute in Time" by Hayden Carruth from *The CEA Critic" 48:3 (Spring 1986)* by permission of the *CEA Critic.* ©College English Association, Inc.

THE SEWANEE REVIEW: "Poet in Eclipse" was first published in *The Sewanee Review* 99 (Fall 1991). Copyright © 1991 by Louis D. Rubin, Jr. Reprinted by permission of the editor.

PACH BROS, NY for cover photograph of Karl Shapiro.

LAYLE SILBERT: Photograph: copyright © by Layle Silbert.

HELEN LUNDEEN WHITTEMORE: For two pictures, number 6 and 7, taken in Washington on the occasion of the 40th anniversary celebrations of the Consultants in Poetry to Congress